The Language of Love, Forgiveness, Faith, Prayer and Healing

How to walk in holiness and harness the power of daily miracles.

Leon Gosiewski

Onwards and Upwards Publishers, Berkeley House,
11 Nightingale Crescent, West Horsley, Surrey KT24 6PD

www.onwardsandupwards.org

First published by Community Ministries in 2010.
Second edition published in 2011.

Scripture quotations are taken from the Revised Standard Version of the
Bible, copyright 1952 [2nd edition, 1971] by the Division of Christian
Education of the National Council of the Churches of Christ in the
United States of America. Used by permission. All rights reserved.

ISBN: 978-1-907509-35-3
Cover design: Leah-Maarit

Printed in the UK

Dedication

In loving memory of my dad, Fabian, and my wife's mother, Mary Dobney.

Acknowledgements

With heartfelt thanks to those nearest to my heart whom I love deeply and who in return love me, forgive me and show so much patience toward me:
Chrissy, Joanna, Sarah & Liz

- And -

My sincere thanks to
Adam, George & Gwen for their help.

Thank you to Chrissy, Sarah and Liz who have read and commented on my manuscripts. Thank you also to Chrissy for the many hours spent reading my work, sharing thoughts and ideas, organising the printing of the first edition and, above all, supporting me at every stage with love, understanding, patience and dedication.

About Chasing Your Dreams and Renewed Life Healing Ministries

In partnership with New Life Ministries, Chasing Your Dreams is a unique international healing, coaching, counselling and teaching organisation dedicated to personal development by releasing blocks that prevent healing, health, fitness and holiness. The mandate behind this work is that the blind shall see, the deaf shall hear and the prisoner shall be set free.

Our aim is to reach into local communities, to meet people at their point of need. Have you found a block in your life? A block in healing? A block in health? A block in fitness? A block in knowing God? Does your block prevent you from being positive and releasing your potential? Chasing Your Dreams Ministries is dedicated to inspiring, challenging and helping you to unlock amazing and wonderful discoveries, your daily miracles released through the power of God as you walk in love, blessing and holiness.

We believe that if miracles do not happen there is something wrong. The integrity and principles by which we work are non-denominationally, biblically based.

"You are what you believe you are."

What do you believe your potential is? Are you held back by negative beliefs? Is your faith in need of activation?

In this book, I explore how what we say, what we think and what we believe unlocks the miracles that a loving God has always intended and longs to release in our lives so that we can bless others.

Background

The founder of Chasing Your Dreams and Renewed Life Healing community ministries is Leon Gosiewski who has spent over thirty years in sport and fitness education. Having witnessed the healing touch of God and then lived many unfruitful years in the 'wilderness', Leon has sought answers to a number of faith questions. Chasing Your Dreams Ministries will not shirk or hide from hard, scrutinising questions, not least of which is "How can negativity be replaced with positivity in our lives?", "What has happened to everyday healing miracles?", "Where has the power gone to attain our dreams?"

Through faith in God combined with caring and compassionate healing, coaching and teaching, Chasing Your Dreams Ministries will help to remove blocks that prevent you from achieving your needs and unlock your potential, bringing a fresh look at God and His promises.

Author's Note

In obedience to God and with genuine, heartfelt love in the name of Jesus the integrity of this book is based upon the Word of God and covered with prayer that it will bless those who read these pages. Details have been checked, but if there are any inaccuracies with any story contained in these pages please let us know so that alterations can be made in any subsequent reprint that may take place.

Contents

Preface

The inspiration behind this publication is based upon the following prophecy:

There is coming a fresh wave of God's power and we are right now at the very brink, the start of this revival that will outstretch any other revival. It will be worldwide and based upon the word of God, dedication to prayer, the power of the Holy Spirit and love reaching into local communities.

God will seek out those who will boldly teach the undiluted word with compassion and love. A fresh breed of pastor will protect the flock, seek out the lost and wandering, and the church will become a house of prayer both as a congregation and in homes. Leaders will be challenged to let go of 'their' work and allow God to move by His Spirit. God's people will be released to exercise their God-given gifts and move through local communities, meeting needs in love and the power of the Holy Spirit. The blessings of God will flow and healings will release captives.

- L.G.

In offering their well-intentioned advice, someone said to me recently that what I was saying is "old hat; God does not work like that anymore."

Dear friend, on considering this advice my thoughts were drawn to the God of Malachi 3:6 ("For I the Lord do not change") and Hebrews 13:8 ("Jesus Christ is the same yesterday, today and forever"). This is not a new prophecy, it is not a new revival and it is not a new move of God. All of these things are already contained in God's word, the Bible, but we have drifted away and become divided. God is calling His people to move in harmony.

Through its publications, healing ministry, training of groups and individual coaching sessions, Chasing Your Dreams Community Ministries is seeking to help people at their point of need and open the door to a world of daily miracles, positivity and a loving, powerful God.

This publication is intended to be a teaching springboard for seeking God in a fresh way and a self-help resource that readers can apply to their lives and unlock untold treasures. It is available for you to turn to for growth, inspiration and help, a twenty-four hour aid that offers positive uplifting when difficulties arise and a reminder that there is an all-powerful God who never sleeps. Crucially, throughout this book, readers are pointed toward what the Bible has to say about key life issues. This book is neither a panacea for Christian wellbeing nor a substitute for God's word, the Bible, but rather a thought-provoking guide, always conscious of its weaknesses, fallibility and imperfections.

Take a moment now to prayerfully reflect on your personal, church and fellowship experiences. Do you have a sense deep down of something that is not quite right? Are you challenged and convicted? Are you seeing and experiencing the promises of God? How closely do all of these questions and your experience match what the Bible has to say?

Please understand me, this is not intended to stir up anger. It is not an opportunity to point the finger, to pass blame or to criticise. Rather, this is an opportunity to take a fresh look at what the Bible has to say and at our own responsibilities, and above all to re-set the direction of our daily walk with God so that we are closer to Him than ever before. Samuel said, "Speak Lord for your servant hears" (1 Samuel 3:10). God is calling His people to listen and allow Him to speak.

What has happened is that many churches, ministers and followers have set their compass incorrectly. As any orienteer or navigator will know, if you set your compass one degree out over a short distance it will not make too much difference in locating your destination - all will seem fine - but over a very long distance you will miss your target by a long way. The question is, are we on target?

For many the compass has been set to meet humanistic needs and conform to traditions and explanations, causing them to drift further away from holiness. I have grappled with these problems, seeking answers elsewhere, and as a result fell deeper and deeper into negativity and dead ends. Through my sin I have hurt a number of people who are close to me, but the grace of God is, by His mercy, never failing. The purpose of the grace of God is to bring us to a place of holiness.

The idea for the title of this book came about as a result of a number of linked personal experiences and realisations regarding the little understood power of our words. We have the word of God and we have the words that we use. It suddenly seemed logical that if the two did not match then miracles could not happen. If, on the other hand, they matched then untold treasures would unfold.

May the Holy Spirit take these words and use this publication to lift and revive those who enter in. I pray for the Spirit of revival to be released in mighty power, to the glory of God.

Prologue

Smith Wigglesworth, speaking about the Bible, said:

Never compare this Book with other books. This Book is from heaven. It does not contain the Word of God; it is the Word of God. It is supernatural in origin, eternal in duration and value, infinite in scope and divine in authorship. Read it through! Pray it in! Write it down.

From the very opening words of this book the focus is clearly set upon God and His word, the Bible. The introduction quotes the words of Yorkshire-born 'man of faith' Smith Wigglesworth (1859 – 1947) who encourages us not only to read the Bible but to, what he calls, "pray it in" to the very depths of our being; and by writing it down, as those engaged in education will know, our comprehension, learning and understanding are reinforced. I would presume to go a little further and state, as I am sure Smith Wigglesworth would have confirmed, that we should also seek the help of the Holy Spirit, whom Jesus called in John 15:26 our counsellor, who bears witness to Christ. You may ask why I boldly make this presumption; I do so based upon the words of Ephesians 6:18 which say, "Pray at all times in the Spirit, with all prayer and supplication."

Wigglesworth actually added to his comment about the importance of the Word of God by revealing that he had read no other book than the Bible. I wonder how you feel about that! When I read this quotation I was amazed because for one reason or another I had out of necessity read many books covering all sorts of topics as part of my training. In the course of these many readings, mixed with useful and informative information, I have also come across much that has been unhelpful, conflicting and, shockingly, a lot that has proved to be just plain wrong or deceptive. In these respects, and for spiritual reasons, I feel that Smith was in an extremely fortunate position. Having said this, we could get the impression that he was living in a lucky period of history when the demand and need for exposure to so much academia was not so necessary, particularly for a career, and therefore it was easier to avoid. We get a sense of Smith's deliberate act, however, when we learn that he would not even allow a newspaper to enter his home! Even if Smith were alive today, his approach would be no different. You see, Smith Wigglesworth understood something that many of us have totally missed. He understood that what enters one's mind can make or destroy a person. He understood the intense warfare waged over our minds and that Satan, just like any fighting force in a battle, attacks us at our most vulnerable point. Our eyes, ears, minds and thoughts are key assets, but they are also our most vulnerable points. Smith was totally aware of the battlefield lines and that walking with God means reading His word and communing with Him in prayer in order to build a wall around our mind to ward off Satan and live in God's power.

As far as anything that we read about God and Christian living is concerned, there can never be a substitute for the Bible, the inspired word of God. It is a resource specifically given to us by God that provides teaching materials for our edification and growth. It reproves and corrects our thinking and actions and it is the source of our training in righteousness; or, put another way, it is a guide for walking a life that has God's seal of approval and is pleasing to Him. That is why in this book reference is continually made to what the Bible says and readers are consistently encouraged to prayerfully, in the Spirit, search and check all things in light of what God's Word has to say.

It is a modern day travesty that the Church has been caught up in a two-pronged attack that has deflected the word of God from penetrating the hearts and souls of mankind.

The first pitfall is based upon a lack of knowledge and application of the word of God, which leaves us open to misguidance, illustrated in the temptations of Jesus found in Matthew 4:5-7 where Satan demonstrates how to manipulate the scriptures so that the truths contained within them are misquoted.

Satan begins by attempting to cast seeds of doubt, saying "if". Next he shows that he is well versed in what the Bible says; he makes reference to the scriptures, in this instance misquoting the words of Psalm 91:11, saying, "He will give his angels charge of you" and "on their hands they will bear you up, lest you strike your foot against a stone." The actual verse says, "For He will give His angels charge of you to guard you in all your ways. On their hands they will bear you up, lest you dash your foot against a stone."

14

Jesus, guarded in all his ways, gives a response to the temptation based on Deuteronomy 6:16: "You shall not put the Lord your God to the test."

The second pitfall is that of watering down the scriptures in an attempt to soften the blow of their impact and to avoid upsetting hearers in case they will not come to church. The result has been devastating to the church, with numbers falling year on year, and the impact has weakened thousands of lives as Christians are not made aware of vital messages or only partial knowledge is imparted. This demonstrates a need to study God's word and pray it into the depths of our heart.

This book is not about watering down the gospel and Christian message, nor does it focus on glorifying anyone or anything other than God. The message from the scriptures is clear. If whatever we read, see or hear about Christian living and walking with God does not measure up against the Bible then it should be discarded; otherwise there is a real and present danger of falling into the trap of compromise and deception.

Why do I say this in such straightforward and uncompromising terms? Paul, talking about the danger of false teaching says:

2 Corinthians 11:3

I am afraid that as the serpent deceived Eve by his cunning, your thoughts will be led astray from a sincere and pure devotion to Christ.

If we consider this logically, what other source of guidance and teaching from God do we have? What other yardstick do we have for walking with God? What basis does any man have for teaching from the pulpit, stage, books, radio, television, computer or any other communicational means something that is contrary to the Bible or has no godly substance?

If there is one message that this book aims to highlight it is that in these last days, before the return of Christ, there is a targeted and concerted spiritual war taking place in the churches for the minds of the people; increasingly this is affecting leaders who teach God's word and influence those to whom they minister. They are being caught up in this deception, weakening the church and hindering the purposes of God.

Please bear with me for this is not an easy message or one said in an uncaring and light-hearted manner. If what is being taught from the platform or pulpit does not measure up against the scriptures it should set off 'alarm bells' and cause us to run in order to find spiritual homes where the word of God is undiluted.

Paul, writing to Timothy in his second letter, was deeply concerned about the need to preach sound biblical doctrine and so he wrote:

2 Timothy 4:3,4
For the time is coming when people will not endure sound teaching, but having itching ears they will accumulate for themselves teachers to suit their own likings, and will turn away from listening to the truth and wander into myths.

Sadly this is a place that many have come to, and many will no doubt throw their hands up at what they are reading here. Dear friend, we need to guard what we allow to settle in our minds because that which fills our minds drips into our heart, the very core of our being. This is one of the reasons why we read these words:

Luke 6:45
The good man out of the good treasure of his heart produces good, and the evil man out of his evil treasure produces evil; for out of the abundance of the heart his mouth speaks.

It is important to consider what settles deep in our hearts because what is in our hearts will issue from our mouths. This message is worth reiterating: access to that which is in our hearts is gained through our minds, and so, as Solomon was trying to explain, we need to be vigilant over our hearts and guard them:

Proverbs 4:23
Keep your heart with all vigilance; for from it flow the springs of life.

Paul warns about being deceived:

1 Corinthians 15:33

Do not be deceived: 'Bad company ruins good morals'.

We simply cannot allow ourselves to take in unfruitful messages on television, in the papers, at nightclubs, over the World Wide Web, and so on. The truth of the matter is, these messages and bad company will take their toll upon us. We fool ourselves if we think that we are immune and untouchable. If we 'play with fire' we will get burnt; we are deceived or we deceive ourselves if we think otherwise. Philippians 4 tells us what we should be doing:

Philippians 4:8

Finally brethren, whatever is true, whatever is honourable, whatever is just, whatever is pure, whatever is lovely, whatever is gracious, if there is any excellence, if there is anything worthy of praise, think about these things.

As we seek to rid the sin and darkness from our hearts, we can be assured that it is possible to work towards doing so. As James explains, what we need to do is:

2 Corinthians 10:5

Draw near to God and He will draw near to you. Cleanse your hands, you sinners, and purify your hearts, you men of double mind.

We have the ability to change what is in our hearts by walking with God and taking every thought captive in order to obey Christ.

This book considers the language that we use related to some key areas of our Christian lives. Why consider the language that we use? If it is not evident yet, this is best summarised by linguist and philosopher Avram Noam Chomsky who is reported as saying, "Language is a mirror of the mind." In other words, what we say is a reflection of our inner thoughts and beliefs, the real person that we are.

There is a link between what we say, our physiology and the powerful affect that our words can have upon ourselves and others. This will be explored in these pages through the qualities of love, forgiveness, faith, prayer and healing, in order to inspire, stimulate and help you to open the door to something wonderful happening in your life - daily miracles and holy living.

In each of the Christian life experiences covered in these pages, the focus is toward what we say internally and externally, the type of language or words that we use and how our words are a reflection of what is going on in our thoughts and beliefs. These words then translate into, and are expressed through, our behaviour and actions or, put simply, the person that we become and truly are.

There is no pretension intended or implied in this book. I fully recognise, first and foremost, that these are words that God is speaking to me; you are therefore simply invited to share with me on my journey of discovery and learning. At the same time, these will be life-changing messages that will help us together to find the heart of God. The messages contained herein are not easy. They are not written lightly but rather in faithfulness. The focus is on Jesus Christ; there is no intentional dilution of the gospel and God's word, which is ultimately the benchmark that all teaching must be measured against.

In the first section we will look at the fundamental importance that the Bible places on love and the influence and power of love in and on our daily living. Understanding and walking in love - love for God, love for others, and love for (and acceptance of) ourselves being the first steps toward unlocking untold treasures and a special relationship with God.

Just as a dysfunctional family distorts the love, support, respect and safety of its members, so a dysfunctional relationship with God distorts the depths that we can attain. The point I am trying to make here is that if we do not truly love God then we will not be able to establish a proper relationship with Him even though He does His part. This in turn affects our trust and confidence so that we do not exercise it as we should. You see, knowing God's love is one thing, but actually living in it, being bathed in it and being released by it is a very different place to be. Perfect love casts out fear of punishment. If we walk in fear, if we beat ourselves up over mistakes, our love is not perfected.

Consider for a moment: when we love someone, we have complete confidence in them. We place our trust in him or her. We know that they will do as they promise. God is holding His hands out to us, inviting us to come to Him. The decision to become fully functional, to love God and to completely trust and put our faith in Him, is ours. The bottom line here is that a lack of faith in God is an indicator of our true relationship and how much we actually love God. Would my dad have let me down? I can emphatically and confidently say, "No!" How much more then can I totally trust God!

We discover in this chapter why love is so important, how it affects every aspect of our lives, how to love God, others and ourselves, and what the fruits of love produce. Amongst many other things, love is a springboard to faith.

Following on from the Christian message of love, we will naturally move in chapter two to another central message of God's word: the question of forgiveness. This forms the essence of the New Testament message, from God's example of forgiving our sins through to our forgiveness of those that sin against us.

We will discover here the all too often glossed-over, harder-edged side of what it truly means to walk in obedience to God. Obedience in forgiveness does not come easily or without cost. It requires that we humble ourselves before the mighty hand of God, whilst the alternative only injects the corrosive and destructive acid of unforgiveness, resulting in a costly account on our lives.

In Matthew 6:9-15, Jesus teaches us how to pray through the Lord's Prayer, and in verses 14 and 15 He goes on to say that if we forgive others then God will forgive us but if we do not forgive those who sin against us then neither will God forgive us! This may not be a message that we want to hear, but it is a reality. It is not only an act of obedience but also one of demonstrable love; in addition it is a prerequisite to faith and prayer.

The third chapter will take us on an exploration of faith, for without faith it is impossible to please God. Faith, as we will have discovered in the first chapter, is developed out of a love for God. Our daily communication with Him and, importantly, exercise of our faith is built on the bedrock of a special relationship with God. In this chapter we will also examine areas of misunderstanding and incorrect teaching concerning faith and how we can harness its power.

Throughout history soldiers have worn breastplates; today we call them flak jackets or vests, also sometimes known as body armour or ballistic vests. The purpose of these vests is to protect the vulnerable upper body; in our modern day protection can be from knife attack, gunshots, flying debris or shrapnel. The Christian can also be protected with a breastplate from the vulnerable stealth attacks and 'shrapnel' that life and Satan fling at us. This breastplate protection that we can put on is described in 1 Thessalonians 5:8 as faith and love; this is why we will begin this book with these two essential qualities.

In building a relationship with God by loving Him and placing our confidence in Him through a love that is expressed by faith, the next chapter examines our daily communication through the power of prayer and what it is to prayer prayers that touch the very heart of God.

Just as any fighting force needs to stay in communication with its supply lines and strategic instructions, so we need to communicate not just daily but continually with God.

Prayers are a daily conversation in and through the Holy Spirit in which we recognise who God is, thank Him for His faithfulness, talk through our needs, seek advice, share our thoughts, listen intently and build our relationship. It is like having a friend with whom we can share anything, talk together, listen to one another and receive guidance from. Our prayer channel is a two-way, 24/7 relationship. It is not about us doing all of the talking. Prayer, crucially, involves listening and allowing God to speak.

The fact is, when we love someone we want to be with them; we want to talk with them for hours on end. Time just seems to stop as we are caught up in their presence. In the same way, a deep and sincere love for God will cause us to spend time communing with Him.

Finally, we will visit one of the promises of God: healing. Again we will chip away misconceptions and the various misunderstandings that surround healing and the healing ministry. This will lead us to consider the pitfall of deceptions that rob us of receiving all that God has to offer. Our understanding that sickness is of Satan will bring us to a point where we can open ourselves to God, allowing Him to take our lives and to bring healing into our bodies. Healing is God's gift of deliverance, which is, at its best, accompanied by righteousness and holiness. What better way can we demonstrate our love and compassion to others than to express God's love as channels of healing miracles?

In concluding, we will realise that our walk through love, forgiveness, faith, prayer and healing not only releases the power of God and the work of the Holy Spirit in our lives but also leads us along the road toward righteousness and holiness without which we cannot see God.

We will come to a realisation that holiness is time spent with God to the point where His influence and role modelling become a part of who we are. It is about thinking God's will, speaking God's will, believing God's will, and acting in God's will, immersing ourselves in (and walking by) the Holy Spirit.

1. The Language of Love

*Life is meaningless only if we allow it to be. Each of us has the power to
give life meaning, to make our time and our bodies and our words into
instruments of love and hope.*

- Tom Head -

Introduction

Why love? I cannot express this more succinctly than through the
famous and often quoted words of 1 Corinthians 13:

1 Corinthians 13:13
So faith, hope, love abide, these three; but the greatest of these is love.

Love is described as the greatest of the three key qualities mentioned
in this scripture, even above faith which, according to Hebrews 11:6, we
cannot please God without! The importance of love has never struck me
in quite that way before: love is greater than faith in its quality! Please do
not misunderstand; this is not saying that we can have, and walk in, love
and that faith is not necessary; rather, as we will learn later, these two great
qualities complement one another.

During the course of this section we will, perhaps unusually for this
type of book, look at love from several viewpoints and angles. In doing so
the heart of God will reach as many people as possible; those reading
these words will be able to connect with the message from their own
experience, not just 'in word' but also as a fresh release of the impact that
true love has for us, no matter who we are.

So why exactly is so much importance placed upon love? This
crucial question leads us into an area that has unfortunately received little
or insufficiently focussed attention, leaving many in its silence bereft of
the depth, richness and reality of true, God-given love. The experience of
love for many simply does not exist because, as I know from my own
upbringing, love was not something that flowed easily, whilst
condemnation and feelings of unworthiness prevailed. It was not through

personal experience that I knew or could in real terms describe or express love, and perhaps worse still, I did not know how to receive love. The danger here is that those who experience this in their lives can end up, as I did, seeking love in the wrong places and ways; or for some, as a defence mechanism, they turn cold and hard and even bitter, neither of which state brings fulfilment.

If you are a person who has been brought up in a loving environment, you are in a most privileged position; fully understanding God's love will very likely come far more easily and naturally to you because you have been and are loved for *who* you are and not *what* you are. For those who have not experienced love, the comprehension behind being loved, especially as someone who has messed up, made mistakes and acted in sin, is foreign because your experience is that punishment and fear are most often the consequence. Feelings and experiences of having not earned or deserved love need considerable enlightenment and revelation, not to mention healing. Many people are in this trapped position, and that is why the message of God's love is so important and the path to salvation made wide open.

The love of God has a way of melting even the hardest person and softening the harshest of circumstances. It is through love that the children of God can minister to friends, family, neighbours and colleagues, blessing them in their prayers and humbling themselves before them and God.

Love is not simply a word; it is expressed through action, and it is an overwhelming feeling. To speak of love yet to act outside of love is a trait that is all too often experienced. Words of love must also carry with them actions of love. Otherwise the words do not correspond to love at all but to desire, lust or infatuation. The action of love creates feelings of love and harmony. The absence of the action of love creates feelings of fear and disharmony.

The fact is, love is a commandment and a pre-requisite to Christian living and walking in righteousness. In 1 John 4:7-21 we have some colourful descriptions and statements about love and its source. In verse 21 we read:

1 John 4:21

...and this commandment we have from him, that he who loves God should love his brother also.

In the previous verse a very strong statement is made, saying that if we say we love God and then do not show this love to others, it is a lie. In fact, verse 8 states that if we do not love, we do not know God, for God is love. These are uncompromisingly strong and extremely powerful words which reflect the seriousness and importance that God places upon love.

If the Bible is making such a strong and passionate statement, then it is a sure sign that we are dealing with something that is close to the heart of God who is, after all, the very essence of love. This is a subject that therefore requires our close attention as we examine ourselves in the process.

Our natural reactions and thoughts may be less than loving and so, in our weakness, we are thrown into total reliance upon God, asking that He, in His divine wisdom and power, will give us the heart of Jesus. Indeed this should be our prayer request. We can ask God to release in us a love that sees others as God sees them, to feel about others the way that God feels about them and to think about others as God thinks about them. It is when we receive God's love and walk in it that we can love others as He loves us.

It may be true for many of us that we really do not know what love is. How many of us honestly know the love that God has for us? How many of us have really experienced that 'leap' in our heart and depth of indescribable feeling that comes from realising just how much God actually does love us - that is, you and me - just as we are, warts and all?

As I think on these things, I am reminded how I felt when watching the Mel Gibson film 'The Passion of the Christ'. Now, I will not comment on the accuracy of the film, but there was one scene that made me almost shout out loudly, "Stop!" The lashings and beatings depicted were so severe, so prolonged, that I just wanted them to finish. I could not take it anymore. This picture of the suffering that Christ endured for me was so real and yet, if I am honest, totally incomprehensible. I do not deserve such an outpouring of love; I have let God down so many times and yet

His faithfulness, His love endures. This is a 'love above loves' in which God has never condemned me.

The truth is, it is comparatively easy for people to do good deeds out of personal need or for personal acclaim and recognition or to think that love is something that is achieved through good works. In Luke 6, Jesus talks about the law of love and he makes a statement that demonstrates the unconditional aspects of Godly love:

Luke 6:32-34

If you love those who love you, what credit is that to you? For even sinners love those who love them. And if you do good to those who do good to you, what credit is that to you? For even sinners do the same. And if you lend to those from whom you hope to receive, what credit is that to you? Even sinners lend to sinners to receive as much.

Contained in these words Jesus outlines that 'extra mile' that separates God's love and God's people from others. This love is extended freely and unconditionally; and it is mine, it is yours, ripe for accepting and taking.

God knows however that we must first be loved, know love and walk in love before we can truly express it. Love naturally produces love-reactions from the depths of our very being; we just cannot help ourselves. Even if something bad happens, we love.

If you want to test your love status, observe how you react to situations that affect you personally when someone does something to upset or offend you. Now take these actions and reactions to the mercy seat of God, and ask Him daily to love through you and empower you to love as He loves.

These words, said to be adapted from the writings of American writer Dr. Kent M. Keith when he was nineteen, were reportedly found on Mother Teresa's wall:

People are often unreasonable, irrational, and self-centred.
Forgive them anyway.

If you are kind, people may accuse you of selfish, ulterior motives.

Be kind anyway.

If you are successful, you will win some unfaithful friends and some genuine enemies.
Succeed anyway.

If you are honest and sincere people may deceive you.
Be honest and sincere anyway.

What you spend years creating, others could destroy overnight.
Create anyway.

If you find serenity and happiness, some may be jealous.
Be happy anyway.

The good you do today will often be forgotten.
Do good anyway.

Give the best you have, and it will never be enough.
Give your best anyway.

In the final analysis, it is between you and God.
It was never between you and them anyway.

I have to hold my hands up here and confess my failings. It is at this point that I honestly and seriously feel that I should stop, and yet an inner conviction leads me to continue and to share a journey of discovery, fulfilment and breakthrough together with you. This is in many ways a strange and perhaps unique place to find oneself. I pray therefore that in His infinite wisdom God will anoint and bless these words and those who read this message of love.

Having reached this point we encounter a strange paradox and irony. We know that love is something that is not given because it is deserved or earned. Those to whom much is forgiven, who do not know love, are those who treasure it all the more. It begs the question then: how can we truly know the reality of God's love and walk in it? We read:

2 John 1:6

This is love, that we follow his commandments; this is the commandment, as you have heard from the beginning, that you follow love.

How do we follow love? We read:

1 John 2:5

Whoever keeps his word, in him truly love for God is perfected.

And again:

1 John 4:12

No man has ever seen God; if we love one another, God abides in us and His love is perfected in us.

We have, encapsulated in these scripture verses, the road of love. Its way is to immerse ourselves in the word of God, to obey His commandments, humble ourselves and to simply 'just do it' - to love. It is not about feelings. God's love is more than feelings and 'doing things because we want to' whilst denying those that cause us grief.

Take a look at what Jesus did in the garden of Gethsemane. He was being arrested and taken, as he knew full well, to be ill treated, flogged and crucified and yet he healed one of the guards of the high priest whose ear had been cut off! What an astonishing act of compassion in circumstances far beyond anything you or I will probably ever face. What we witness is the love and compassion that Christ, with all of his powerful resources and God-given abilities demonstrated throughout his ministry.

Take a few moments to consider these scripture verses:

1 Corinthians 13:1

If I speak in the tongues of men and of angels, but have not love, I am a noisy gong or a clanging cymbal.

1 Corinthians 13:2

If I have prophetic powers, and understand all mysteries and all knowledge, and if I have all faith, so as to remove mountains, but have not love, I am nothing.

1 Corinthians 13:3

If I give away all I have, and if I deliver my body to be burned, but have not love, I gain nothing.

John 15:13,14

This is my commandment, that you love one another as I have loved you. Greater love has no man than this that a man lay down his life for his friends. You are my friends if you do what I command you.

What we learn here is that love is 'keeping God's word and commandments'; it is having love for God and for one another and laying down our lives for other people; it is about doing what God commands through trust and obedience. Jesus was not only trusting and obedient to God; he actually laid down His life in love for you and for me. It is difficult in many ways to comprehend this sacrifice, but Jesus, through his actions, has literally saved our lives from certain death. Jesus considered you and me - imperfections, failings and denials and everything else that you can mention - worth dying for.

The other question that we may ask is: how do we know that we are successfully walking in love? What is the benchmark that we can use? If we turn to Matthew 22, Jesus answers us through a question that was originally intended to test Him:

Matthew 22:36-40

"Teacher, which is the great commandment in the law?" And He said to him, "'You shall love the Lord your God with all of your heart, and with all of your soul, and with all of your mind.' This is the first commandment. And a second is like it, 'You shall love your neighbour as yourself'. On these two commandments depend all the law and the prophets."

In providing this answer, Jesus basically condensed the first four of the Ten Commandments into love for God and the second six into love for others. Fulfilling the Ten Commandments is therefore our benchmark for love. How do I know this? Take a look at what Paul had to say:

Romans 13:8-10

Owe no one anything, except to love one another; for he who loves his neighbour has fulfilled the law. The commandments, 'You shall not commit adultery, You shall not kill, You shall not steal, You shall not covert' and any other commandment, are summed up in this sentence, 'You shall love your neighbour as yourself'. Love does no wrong to a neighbour; therefore love is the fulfilling of the law.

Love is at the very heart of the Commandments, a powerful force that lies within the capability of all of us. We all have the capacity to love and, as we can see from the opening quotation, each of us can 'give life meaning' through the words we use and the actions we take expressed in and through love. Love is an amazing gift - freely available and freely given simply by the words we speak and, more importantly, the actions we take.

The motivation that we have to help others rests purely upon love. Perfect love means that there is no expectation of something in return, no selfishness, ambition, duty or pride and, above all, there is no resentment, hate or unforgiveness in our hearts. Words and actions that come from a heart of love will be powerful and forceful; they will convict to the very core those who listen. The same words and actions that come from a heart that is not pure in love will offend, and the power, effect and conviction will be lost.

In the introduction to this book, I mentioned the quotation by linguist and philosopher Avram Noam Chomsky who said, "Language is a mirror of the mind." He was succinctly expressing that what we say is a reflection of our inner self - the real person that we are - reflected by our thoughts, beliefs, spoken words and behaviour. I don't know about you, but that puts a whole new perspective and responsibility on what I am daily communicating not only to others but also to myself. Why do I say this? Well, there is another aspect to consider: what we say, think and believe is a direct communication to our own physiology and wellbeing. Yes, what we think and say is a direct command to our body, health and wellness. The language of love has suddenly taken on a new focus: love is a powerful, positive healing force, not only as it is freely given to others but also in its healing power on you and me. The wonderful fact is that as love is given it also gives in abundant measure.

Armed with these new revelations I cannot help but feel empowered, warm and eager to know more about the secrets of love and to be a person of love.

Because one of the ways in which love is communicated is through what we say and how we say it, we will naturally focus our attention in this chapter on the type of language that we use, what we think and say about love and how 'where our love words are rooted' affects the way in which our beliefs, thoughts, words and actions make us who we are.

As I sat in my study to ponder what I was going to say about love, it suddenly dawned on me that not only was this going to be a task with far more challenges, far more depth and far more potential impact than I had first thought, but also that I myself, a person of imperfections, would be challenged to be a man of love in words and deeds. I am actually in the most privileged and precious position of sharing my love through this publication, but I am equally in a vulnerable position because if my love is not perfected it will fail to come across in the written word and fail to touch those who are reading.

What I am sharing is therefore on the one hand something that I hope will inspire and stir you to want to check and research more for yourself from the Bible whilst on the other hand a challenge to the very people that you and I are. It is not about words on a page but an attitude of mind and a life-changing experience. By the end of reading this chapter our lives will be following the road of love - if we choose to go that way.

You are invited to share with me a journey of discovery in two parts, along with its expectancies, emotions and challenges - a journey that I believe we will both enjoy and learn much from, as well as one that we can potentially look back and reflect upon with a sense of joy, fulfilment, hope and, of course, love.

Love is a powerful, consuming feeling and emotion, expressed through our thoughts, words and actions. For love to be love, our thoughts and words must match our actions and the outward display of our emotions which captivate and infect the loved.

In part one, in order to gain a deeper understanding and perspective of love, we will briefly look at the difficulties and complexities of communication and the language and meaning of love as well as why we need love. Having explored these issues we will consider several aspects of love including its spirituality and unconditional qualities.

On entering part two we will consider a number of challenges in pursuit of attaining and being a person of love before closing with meditations on love that will help us and our words to become instruments of love.

PART ONE

Love – A Journey of Discovery

Language is a learned symbolic communication system. By symbolic I mean in terms of the meanings given to the sounds and nuances ascribed to them by the user and receiver. Of course, as we have all realised at some time or another, the interpretation of the language that we use does not always match the other person's interpretation. If you add the fact that some words are highly emotionally charged and then combine this with the way in which speech is delivered, you have a potentially explosive situation for good or for bad, whether intentionally or unintentionally meant. This is precisely why words are so frequently insufficient of their own; they have to be supported by our actions and the love that oozes from our countenance.

Communication breaks down if we are unable to understand what another person is saying. For example, taking an extreme illustration, if I said, "The dichotomous pulchritude of the anas platyrhynchos gender favours in the view of some the male," would I be making any sense? To some, yes; to others, yes and they would correct the context and grammar; to others, in part; and still to others, absolutely not. So that no one is left totally confused, basically what this means is that the beauty between the male and female mallard duck favours, in the view of some, the male duck. Ultimately the meaning of our communication is what others understand or interpret. Love is one of those words that may mean different things to different people and it can of course be misunderstood. It is about sensitivity and an encounter with those, or that, to which it is being expressed.

Another issue to consider is that some of the language that we use has changed its meaning over time or even within certain circles of society. I can remember a few years ago, when whilst teaching a group of sixteen-year-old girls, two said to me concerning a young trainee physical education teacher that he was 'fit'. Their interpretation of fit (handsome) was somewhat different from mine, so I replied, "Don't you think that I am fit?" (meaning 'healthy and agile'). You can imagine the laughter as well as how silly and out of touch I felt.

So, what of this word 'love'? Today the English language uses one word for love and it is one of those words that can mean different things to different people in different situations and circumstances as well as one that can be emotionally highly charged and has changed its meaning over time.

In order to illustrate this point, take a moment to consider the following two questions:

- What does love mean to you?
- What feelings, if any, well up from within you when you think about love?

If you are able, go and ask another person the same questions and compare the results.

What Does The Word Love Mean?

The sorts of responses to the question "What does love mean to you?" may include...

- ...love of the countryside or sea.
- ...love of travel or a vehicle.
- ...love of cream cakes or other foods.
- ...love of the theatre or music etc.
- ...love of a children, brother or sister or other family member.
- ...love of a partner.
- ...love as in sexual desire.
- ...love of a hobby or sport.
- ...love of God.

These example responses and the many more that you may have expressed are so very different and cover a wide range of meaning. Interestingly, in some of these examples reference is made to inanimate objects, and so we have to ask, is it truly possible to love an inanimate object? Well, clearly, if love is about an attachment, a desire or a fondness, then a level of love might be possible; it all depends on how you interpret love! This thought also leads us to consider: is love about *someone* or *something?* We may also ask, "Do I love *you* or do I love your *personality qualities?*" Indeed, "Is this love, or is it infatuation, desire or lust?" We perhaps do not stop sufficiently often enough to think about these questions that only we ourselves can answer until it is too late. The problem is that our emotions are powerful and often rule our heads, and in any case do we really know what love is anyway?

Our thinking has now led us to unravel an aspect of love, suggesting that there are different levels of love which, for our purposes here, I will simply refer to in no particular hierarchical order as...

- ...the spiritual level.
- ...the love of others level.
- ...the mankind level.
- ...the relationship level.
- ...the physical or sexual level.
- ...the inanimate level.

Whatever labels may be given or however the levels are graded, what we can see is that love in one form or another impacts on every aspect of our lives, and in this sense it is no wonder that we may find it difficult to express what love is.

If we turn to the dictionary for help to find out what love means, we discover that there are several additional and enriched interpretations, such as...

- ...to have a great attachment to and affection for.
- ...to have passionate desire, longing and feelings for.
- ...to like or desire to do something.
- ...an intense emotion of affection, warmth, fondness and regard toward a person or thing.

The word love is descriptive of one of the most powerful and forceful experiences in our lives. For most of us it will be a positive experience and for others it may be tinged with negative overtones - of a broken love or a false love, and so on.

Whatever your personal experiences of love may be, they are, as we have already discovered, emotionally charged. If you are one of those who have experienced hurt through what you had thought was love then I gently and carefully offer you a heartfelt observation that might help you: broken love, false love and negative love are not love at all. In none of our interpretations, descriptions or definitions do we find love to be a negative thing unless we add a negative prefix or suffix word, which actually then, by definition, negates love and is not love at all.

Of course, it may be that you have experienced a 'falling out of love' and this may be painful; but again, true love does not refer to a falling out, a loss or a taking away of love, and these are not therefore love. God's love is not changeable. He does not 'fall out of' or take away His love or make it conditional. Sin separates us from God and clouds the feelings that we may experience because of our own guilt. Sin may build a barrier between us and God and create fear in us, but God's love for each one of us as individuals never changes; that is why we can come in repentance and be so easily forgiven. God respects our decision to separate ourselves from Him, but it is not what He wants for us; it hurts Him, but it does not stop His love for us. If we choose alienation from God and separation in order to do our own thing it is our choice; it is not God's perfect plan for us and so to say that God does not love us is to deny and shirk our own responsibility, pushing blame away from where it should actually sit - with you and me.

Consider for one moment these words:

John 3:16,17

For God so loved the world [that means you, whoever you are and it means me] that he gave his only son, that whoever believes in him should not perish but have eternal life; for God sent the Son into the world, not to condemn the world, but that the world might be saved through him.

Dear friend, whoever you are, God does not condemn; He loves you and He forgives you. It is Satan who tricks people into sin. It is Satan who brings disasters and illness. It is Satan who accuses. Yes, it is true that we are guilty of sinning, *but* it is Satan who then uses this, saying to us that we cannot be forgiven and that God does not love us. These are outright lies and deceptions. Why do I say this? Take a look at these examples:

- Genesis 3 – We read that Satan accuses God before Adam and Eve.
- Job 1 – Satan accuses Job before God.
- Zechariah 3:1-5 – Satan stands accusing Joshua.
- Matthew 4: 1-11 – Satan tries to tempt and accuse Jesus.
- Revelation 12:10 – "The accuser of our brethren, who stood before God and hurled accusations day and night."

Romans 8: 31-34

What shall we say to this? If God is for us, who is against us? He who did not spare His own son but gave him up for us all, will he not also give us all things with him? Who shall bring any charge against God's elect? It is God who justifies: who is to condemn?

In an attempt to extract as much as we can from the meanings of love, let's dig a little deeper into the origins of this word to see if we can reach into the heart of what it means for us. The English language has been developed from a number of European and Anglo-Saxon influences that led to what was known as the Old English language and later, through to the natural evolution of language with constant revision and adaptation, to its modern day, ever-changing form.

In order to highlight the confusion that evolving language can create, the word for love is said to have originated from the Germanic Sanskrit word *lubh* meaning 'desire', which was then adopted into the Old English word *lufu* meaning 'a deep affection' or 'to be fond of'. The influence of Latin gave to us another word for love, *amor*, meaning 'love, affection, infatuation, and passion', and if we look to the influence of the Greek translation of love we find several different words that express its varied meanings and nuances, as follows:

- *Agape* or *Agapao* – Recognised by many as the highest level of love - a caring, gentle, selfless love, associated with the love God has for His Son and mankind. It is expressed in and through action; it is a dispassionate love not based upon feelings but upon obedience and therefore expressed even if we do not feel like it. Examples in the Bible can be found in John 3:16 ("For God so loved [agape] the world that He gave His only Son") and 1 John 3:16 ("By this we know love [agape], that he laid down his life for us.") These were acts of selflessness and obedience.

- *Eros* – This refers to a relationship - the romantic, passionate type of love. If you rearrange the word Eros you get Rose - the red rose being associated with Valentine's Day.
- *Ludus* – An uncommitted love.
- *Mania* – An obsessive, jealous or possessive love.
- *Philia* or *Phileo* – This word means 'friendship'. It is the type of love that may exist within a family but more typically between friends and includes loyalty. John 5:20: "For the Father loves [phileo] the Son". That friendship and closeness linked them together. Again, we read about Lazarus, the one whom Jesus loved [phileo] or 'was friendly with'. John 11:3: "Lord, he whom you love [phileo] is ill."
- *Pragma* – A practical and mutually beneficial relationship such as that of work colleagues.
- *Storge* – Similar to philia, this is a special bonding and affection like that of a parent for a child and is used to describe family relationship love. Romans 12: 10, 'love (storge) one another with brotherly affection' a devoted type of love
- *Thelema* – A desire to do something

The Bible only speaks of three types of love: *Agape*, *Phileo* and *Storge*. As we have already discussed, the modern English language only uses one word for love but this one word incorporates many of the influences mentioned from the Germanic, Latin and Greek origins which are clumped together; so the word 'love' has many meanings and facets that can only really be defined (or at least a fighting chance of a definition given) within the context in which it is being used at any one time.

To this point we have really looked at the academic and contextual side of love, but of course love is practical and emotional. Although the meanings of love are varied (making it imprecise) - ranging from pleasure, such as my example of a love of cream cakes through to interpersonal affection, such as that of a partner - there are four common themes that can be found running through each explanation of love:

- That love is a positive emotion
- That love is something that is good
- That love is something that we feel
- That love is something that we do

I obviously do not know your situation at this moment in time but the fact is that we are all created to want and need love. This is not surprising because we are made in the image of God (Genesis 1:27) and God is love (1 John 4:8). To appreciate this point more clearly, try honestly answering these questions:

- Do you want to be miserable?
- Do you want to suffer?
- Do you want to be unwanted and unappreciated?

Under normal circumstances none of us want to be miserable or to suffer in any way or to be unwanted and unappreciated; we are not made that way. It may of course be that love brings with it pain and challenges, and I will cover this in part two, but these are such that they can strengthen love or the capacity to love. The point that I am seeking to make is that it is impossible for physical, verbal and/or emotional abuse and negativity to co-exist alongside love.

Why do we need love?

As human beings we possess a survival need. We are after all social beings. We need others around us because we survive both through the use of our intellect and, importantly in this context, through our part in community; we need one another and the support that we give to one another. This is reflected in the fact that the Bible refers to all believers as the "body of Christ" and the "unity of the body" (1 Corinthians 12:12-26).

Love is also necessary in order to fulfil our biological need to reproduce and for mankind to perpetuate; therefore we need to socialise, to be with others, to talk with others, to learn and communicate with them. We also need the love of friends for affirmations. Our friends and our reaching out to God, a higher being, help us to affirm ourselves, to feel good about our identities and to help us to make sense of the world.

There are so many aspects to love that make us human, complete and fulfilled.

Overarching all of these points is the fact that without the love that God has for us we have no hope, and without sharing God's love we cannot bring others to a place of love. The ultimate in love is described, as mentioned earlier, in the following famous scripture verses:

John 3:16-18

For God so loved the world that he gave his only Son, that whoever believes in him should not perish but have eternal life. For God sent the Son into the world, not to condemn the world, but that the world might be saved through him. He who believes in him is not condemned; he who does not believe is condemned already, because he has not believed in the name of the only Son of God.

This "condemnation" is a personal choice of separation from God. To deny God and what Jesus has done to set us free is to condemn ourselves, to make a personal choice to walk away from the love of God by refusing to accept it. There are many who refuse God, only calling on Him in times of trouble or disaster but not wanting to have any commitment or relationship with Him, who turn blame on God instead of looking to themselves and their own decisions and consequences that separate them from love.

The reason why love is such a deep, innate yearning and need is that we 'know' that we are undeserving. Yet to be loved even though we do not deserve it, to be forgiven despite who we are and what we are, touches something deep inside of us. Conversely, when someone resists love, when they do things that they know are wrong and love is shown toward them, the hardhearted person reacts and bulks against the goodness being show to them. Effectively, it is what we might term a reaction that causes the person to 'throw their dummy out of the pram'. Unfortunately, in extreme situations the reaction can be violent and aggressive.

Aspects of Love

To love and to be loved is a natural human need without which we are incomplete. Our wellbeing is affected and we cannot really be happy and joyful. If the truth were known, the longings of our hearts can only be satisfied and met through Jesus, who reaches deeper into the depths of our heart and mind than any other person, action, therapy or anything else.

Love covers many aspects of our lives, emotions and intellectual thinking, so let's take a very brief look at some of these. I am not attempting here to go into any particular depth but rather to whet your appetite and to broaden your perspective.

THE PHILOSOPHICAL ASPECT OF LOVE

The philosophical approach to love typically centres upon questions concerning its nature. Some argue that the emotional aspects of love mean that it is irrational and defies explanation. In some ways that is true; however, the uniqueness of love transcends the rationality argument and is seen as representing human moral excellence expressed through qualities and traits such as affection, compassion, kindness and selflessness.

THE PSYCHOLOGICAL ASPECT OF LOVE

The psychological view of love is that it occurs both mentally, through our thoughts, and socially, through interaction with others. Love in this sense is seen as being formed from a series of component parts which are identified as commitment, compassion, intimacy, passion, and some add trust. Each of these components can combine in multiple ways. For example:

- *Romantic love* – Made up of a combination of compassion and intimacy. This type of love does not include commitment and may be short lived.
- *Companion love* – Combining commitment with intimacy. This is the sort of love between best friends who trust and share close secrets with each other.

- *Consummate love* – That which combines each of the components, such as between a married couple or even found in a long-term relationship.

THE PHYSIOLOGICAL ASPECT OF LOVE

Love is a powerful healing mechanism for our biochemical, emotional, mental and physical needs. Someone once said that love is like a drug; others describe an attraction or love as 'chemistry', and indeed this is a description that would not be too far from the truth in terms of its effect on our physiology.

The best known of the love-related chemicals or psychoactive drugs in the human body is *phenylethylamine* (also referred to as PEA), a neurotransmitter. The chemical is found in chocolate, which has been loosely associated with love or a 'comfort food' as a result. The chemical can boost energy and alertness. It has an effect upon the brain that increases happiness and makes us feel 'alive', and these positive emotions transmit across our entire wellbeing and health. In short, love has a positive and healing impact in and on our bodies.

THE MUSICAL ASPECT OF LOVE

Music can have an incredible and powerful affect on our emotions. The power of music and love, when combined, create a potent force.

Music can relax us, as in restaurants or during massage therapy and meditation, or when helping those in pain or anxiety. It can also stir and stimulate us as in rock festivals or during dramatic film scenes.

The lyrics of songs combined with their music can also stimulate our thoughts and even focus our attention, bringing peace and harmony to flood within us. Take for example the Andrew Lloyd Webber song 'Love Changes Everything' from the musical 'Aspects of Love' sung by Michael Ball. As you read these words, or even play the music, take note of the depth behind what is written and sung.

I am particularly struck by the strength of the words in this song. For example, "Love changes everything, how you live and how you die". What a powerful statement! The notion here is that we can either live lives of love, and the benefits thereof, or fail to reach the potential that awaits us. Love enables us to forgive and it can make us do things that we may otherwise not do.

Again, how apt is the line "Love will turn your world around"! Love can change sadness into joy. It causes people to go out of their way in order to help others and those in love; time seems to stop and they are filled with energy.

The song also expresses that side of love that brings pain - the ache of love, the loss of a loved one or the pain as we see others suffering. As it is so aptly put, love is a powerful force which does indeed "change everything".

THE GODLY ASPECT OF LOVE

The Bible makes mention of three types of love.

Agape.

As mentioned earlier, this is an unconditional, obedient love - the love that God has for mankind and the self-sacrificing love given to everyone by Jesus. Again, the famous example of this is found in John 3:16:

John 3:16

For God so loved [agape] the world, that He gave His only begotten Son, that whoever believes in Him should not perish, but have eternal life.

The ultimate demonstration of love was shown to us through Jesus going to the cross, taking upon himself the beating, punching, lashing and pain of crucifixion. Why? Because Jesus wanted, and wants, to save us from our sinful nature and the self-destruction that it brings with it. He wanted to restore the separation that sin created between God and mankind. Therefore He paid the price, the wage of our sin, for those who accept this gift. What love!

Matthew 5: 44

But I say to you, love your enemies, and pray for those who persecute you.

The unconditional aspect of *agape* love makes it very different from other types of love, which are usually conditional and based upon the

42

reactions of others toward us. This is obedient love; it is not about our feelings. We may feel hard done by and have even experienced ill treatment but our love here is demonstrated through forgiveness.

I cannot put this better than the words of Tracy Carrigan: "I opened the Door of my Heart to Unconditional Love." To know and to be a part of *agape* love is a personal choice. You may say that you are fearful of getting hurt, and yes, there is pain in love. God gave His son and Jesus gave his life, the ultimate example of going through pain and expressing unconditional love. What is the alternative? That we do not love, care and support? That we live with no one close to us? The pain and misery of this existence is far greater. It may be a cliché but the old saying that 'pain comes before pleasure' may have a ring of truth. No one ever said that love was easy. Paradoxically, however, those that love live happier, healthier and more fulfilled lives, having opened their hearts to unconditional love and expecting nothing back, yet being overwhelmed by the rewards that can follow from it.

Philia.

This is the love that exists between very close friends. We see a link between *agape* and *philia* love expressed in 1 Peter:

1 Peter 1:22

Since you have in obedience to the truth purified your souls for a sincere love [philia] of the brethren, fervently love [agape] one another from the heart.

John 11:3

The sisters therefore sent to Him saying, 'Lord, behold he whom you love [philia] is sick'.

Such was the love that Jesus had for his friend that he wept.

Storge.

This is only referred to as the type of love found in family relationships. With the 'family love' meaning, it is also use when speaking of 'the family of believers' - a special bonding and devotion.

Romans 12:10

Be devoted to one another in brotherly [storge], give preference to one another in honour.

Because the English language only uses one word for love, it can be difficult to understand some Bible scriptures without taking a closer look at the original translation or by using a concordance. By way of example, let's look at John 21:

John 21:15-17

Jesus said to Simon Peter, 'Simon, son of John, do you [agape] me more than these?' He said to him, 'Yes, Lord; you know that I [phileo] you.' He said to him, 'Feed my lambs'. A second time he said to him, 'Simon, son of John, do you [agape] me?' He said to Him, 'Yes, Lord; you know that I [phileo] you.' He said to him, 'Tend my sheep.' He said to him the third time, 'Simon, son of John, do you [phileo] me? Peter was grieved because he said to him the third time, 'Do you [phileo] me?' And he said to him, 'Lord, you know everything; you know that I love [phileo] you.'

Jesus asked Peter if he loved Him more than the fish and fishing. The love Jesus was talking about was 'obedient love', doing what was asked even if he did not feel like doing it. Each time Peter replied with a 'friendship love' response; he was desperate to show Jesus that the friendship was sure and deep. To put this into context, in a moment of weakness not long beforehand Peter had denied Jesus. He was desperate to make amends. He missed the point that Jesus was making.

When God says that we are to love Him, it is *agape* love: a willingness to trust, obey and serve even if we do not feel like it. If you want to know whether someone loves God, take a look at John 14:

John 14:15

If you love me, you will keep my commandments.

John 14:21

He who has my commandments and keeps them, he it is who loves me.

John 14:23

If a man loves me, he will keep my word.

Our feelings and emotions are shaped by our thoughts and survival needs. To be isolated from love brings anxiety because we are social beings. Of course, periods of being alone can be cathartic, but if this is prolonged and sustained our natural balance of emotions can drive us into depression and a longing to socialise. Knowing and walking in God's love brings peace.

Within the pages of the Bible we find, opened up and laid bare for us, a broader sense and meaning of what love is. This gives us a role model and also a set of principles leading to a challenging key element concerning love.

THE ROLE MODEL

We find firstly that love is personified, and the Bible states that God is love.

1 John 4:8

The one who does not love does not know God, for God is love.

1 John 4:16

And we have come to know and have believed the love which God has for us. God is love, and the one who abides in love abides in God and God abides in him.

Jesus was our role model.

John 13:14,15

If I then, the Lord and the Teacher, washed your feet, you also ought to wash one another's feet. For I gave you an example that you also should do as I did to you.

A SET OF PRINCIPLES

In order to discover what love is, we must turn to the famous Bible verses on love found in 1 Corinthians 13:

1 Corinthians 13: 1-13

If I speak in the tongues of men and of angels, but have not love, I am only a resounding gong or a clanging cymbal. If I have the gift of prophecy and can fathom all mysteries and all knowledge, and if I have a faith that can move mountains, but have not love, I am nothing. If I give all I possess to the poor and surrender my body to the flames, but have not love, I gain nothing. Love is patient; love is kind. It does not envy, it does not boast, it is not proud. It is not rude, it is not self-seeking, it is not easily angered, it keeps no record of wrongs. Love does not delight in evil but rejoices with the truth. It always protects, always trusts, always hopes, always perseveres.

Love never fails. But where there are prophecies, they will cease; where there are tongues, they will be stilled; where there is knowledge, it will pass away. For we know in part and we prophesy in part, but when perfection comes, the imperfect disappears. When I was a child, I talked like a child, I thought like a child, I reasoned like a child. When I became a man, I put childish ways behind me. Now we see but a poor reflection as in a mirror; then we shall see face to face. Now I know in part; then I shall know fully, even as I am fully known.

And now these three remain: faith, hope and love. But the greatest of these is love.

What we discover in this famous Bible scripture, often used at weddings, are the qualities of love: what love is and what love is not. Take a little while to consider each of these qualities, listed below:

Love Is		Love Is Not	
Patient	Trusting	Envious	Self-Seeking
Kind	Hopeful	Boastful	Angered
Truthful	Persevering	Proud	Unforgiving
Protective	Reliable	Rude	Evil

Every aspect of love rings out positivity. When you are positive, what happens to your physiology and to your mental state? They come to life!

THE CHALLENGE

- We can be good orators with lots of good things to say.
- We can have great insights and knowledge.
- Our faith may be powerful and effective.
- We can give to the poor and needy. We can create charities and work hard to aid others.
- We may even be imprisoned or killed for our beliefs.

None of this will really count if we do not also have love. Our challenge is to make a difference, to love God and to love others, to 'walk the talk'.

PART TWO

Love - The Challenges

Love is not theoretical; it has little meaning or affect without actions. It is a conscious walk and one that may require time and energy in order to change. What follows are a series of challenges that you can use to develop and change your life.

CHALLENGE ONE – FIND LOVE

Many people ask, "How can I find love?" This, dear friend, is the wrong question; it is not a matter of how love is found. The question should be, "Where can I find love?"

- Love is within us. We all have it; we can all show it and demonstrate it.
- Love is infectious. The negative side to this is the misuse of love in which it becomes an infectious disease. The positive side is that when we love others as ourselves it will have an infectious impact, changing those around us.
- Love is in the very heart and nature of God. He does not condemn; He forgives. If we feel condemned and unforgiven by God, it is a sure sign that Satan is standing close by and delivering accusations. Dear friend, God loves and forgives. It is up to us whether we receive this or make our own decision to walk away. Whatever our personal choice, God will keep on loving us.

We need to love ourselves. Many people, because of the way in which they have been brought up or because of traumatic experiences, carry with them love-defence or love-deficiency barriers. These are natural mechanisms that we put in place to protect ourselves against hurt and, in certain circumstances, even abuse and ill treatment. Who can blame someone for protecting themself? Given the same situation, anyone would do the same. It is a personal survival mechanism consisting of barriers that repel attempts to both show and receive love so that the experience of hurt is not repeated. At the same time, however, these barriers remove or steal from an individual a quality of life that is precious.

Deficiencies in loving ourselves can stem from the messages that our parents give to us. These include not hugging, forgetting to support us in events of our lives, and not saying, "I love you." It may be that we are brought up to learn that love is only for others. We then believe that loving ourselves is wrong, that we should only be subservient to others and their needs – even to the extreme of parental or partner abuse, whether this be physical or mental.

The fact is that these are false impositions, lies and deceptions. Each of us is unique, special and precious. There is nothing at all wrong in having a love for ourselves that we also use to love others.

Try the following exercise. Find a place where you can relax and repeat these words:

- I am special.
- I am unique.
- I am worthy of being loved.
- I deserve good things.

Repeat these several times. You may feel a little uncomfortable to begin with, but continue to repeat until you feel more natural about each phrase.

Now take a moment to visualise a time when you did or said something that hurt someone. Once you have that picture, imagine that you have written a description of it on a piece of paper. Now take this paper, ask for forgiveness and see that person forgiving you.

Once you have done this, think of a time when you have said or done something to hurt yourself. Again, write it down and then ask yourself for forgiveness and see yourself as a forgiven person.

Finally, take those pieces of paper to a shredder and see yourself shredding the paper. Feel the warmth and love from that forgiveness and repeat the phrases that you started with.

If similar thoughts return, go through the same process again if necessary, and remember that the choice of what any of us allow ourselves to think about is our own. As a special person you and I no longer accept or entertain these negative deceptions.

CHALLENGE TWO – HEALED TO LOVE

In his book 'The Scientific Basis for the Healing Power of Intimacy' (1997), Dean Ornish states:

> *Love and intimacy are at the root of what makes us sick and what makes us well ... I am not aware of any factor in medicine – not diet, not smoking, not stress, not genetics, not drugs, not surgery – that has greater impact on our quality of life, incidence of illness and premature death from all causes.*

Love has an impact on our quality of life, incidence of illness and premature death. Is that as shocking a statement to you as I find it?

Does love, or the lack of it, have such an impact on our health and causes of sickness? Certainly the way in which we feel - our joy, peace and happiness - is heightened when we are loved and love. If you have experienced unloving situations and moments, how does it affect you, your thinking, your physiology, your happiness? They are all diminished. No wonder this feeling has a negative impact, leading to illness, if it is prolonged.

Before we can truly love we need to clear the blockages preventing the flow of love. These blockages include the habits that we display such as anger, unforgiveness, resentment, fear, anxiety and frustration. The amount of joy and happiness that we have in our lives is proportional to the amount of love that we give and show.

Coming in prayer to God, confessing our feelings and needs, and asking Him to meet these needs by blessing us, loving us and comforting us is a good place to start. We may not feel like doing this, but doing it anyway will bring a sense of calm and God's presence.

What we think, what we say and how we act produce powerful messages not only to those around us but also to ourselves and our physiological condition and health. Put another way, speaking and acting in unloving, negative ways can destroy our health, joy and happiness. Forgiveness of, and for, others and ourselves is the first place to begin on the route to 'living a life of love'.

The challenge here is to seek healing of those things that prevent love, to change the unloving and bad habits of negativity that block the flow of love.

The following are healing exercises that you can try.

1. Unforgiveness strangles love and upsets the natural flow of our body chemical balance, which leads to illness. Forgiveness sets us free of these bondages. If you find yourself having unforgiving thoughts – STOP! Do not allow these to continue. Visualise the upsetting situation and person in a loving scenario, and change your thinking and words to positive, loving ones. Ask God for help. See the suffering of Jesus taking all of our hurts upon him and lifting the darkness away from the situation.

2. If you find yourself going back to things from the past, this brings a cloud of gloom, a bit like the dark clouds of a storm overhead. Visualise the sun shining from the throne of God in heaven with its rays bringing light, warmth and healing to those past memories. Change those images so that they reflect goodness. If it is something someone has said, forgive them and see that situation as healed and forgotten.

3. Visualise yourself like a lamb bouncing across green fields on a sunny day, no care in the world - free, relaxed, at ease, vibrant.

4. Take time to meditate on Jesus and the things that bring you joy, peace and relaxation.

5. Affirm your love. Speak words of love to yourself such as, "I am a person of love", "I show love in all that I say and do", "I am a special person; I am free; I am vibrant". You can say this because God loves you.

6. Ensure that what you read, listen to and watch all edify love.

The love of God is perfect. It brings healing and it lifts infirmities. The next six challenges will help you to make these changes.

CHALLENGE THREE – LOVE GOD

The Pharisees in the time of Jesus were a religious political party, or social group of intellects, that liked to make known their good works and enjoyed the reverence that others gave to them. On one occasion a

Pharisee who was also a lawyer decided to challenge Jesus by testing Him in order to see if he could display his superiority and intellect over Jesus. He asked Jesus if He knew the greatest of the commandments. Jesus answered:

Matthew 22:37,38
You shall love the Lord your God with all your heart, and with all your soul, and with all your mind. This is the great and foremost commandment.

The biblical road to love is firstly to love God. What an awesome privilege! We don't just have 'something' or 'someone' to love; we have God. He loves us, but as with any relationship the choice to reciprocate the fulness of this love is ours.

We have already seen that out of love God gave His son and that out of love Jesus gave his life. He was prepared to go through a great deal of suffering and pain just for you, just for me. I find that difficult to comprehend but that is how much you and I are worth. How much we are loved!

It is a simple and perhaps obvious statement, but love begins by taking the *step* to love. It is an action and commitment that we individually choose to take. Loving God and being loved by God is a personal choice. In God we have a shelter, a refuge and protection, a place of security and confidence.

CHALLENGE FOUR – LOVE OTHERS

Jesus confounded the questioner by saying:

Matthew 22:39,40
The second is like it; you shall love your neighbour as yourself. On these two commandments depend the whole Law and Prophets.

The challenge here is to have the same love regard for others as we would have and want for ourselves. If we would see others in our shoes, wishing them to be treated as we would want to be treated and feel what we would want to feel, our approach would be very different.

CHALLENGE FIVE – PRACTICE LOVE

"How can I demonstrate love?"

When I played sport competitively I was able to succeed to a certain degree because I had a natural gift and talent. This natural ability was put to the test, especially when faced with competitors who were technically and tactically proficient, able to counter and challenge me as an athlete. Being ill-prepared or ill-equipped meant that life was tough in the competitive arena. What I had to do to overcome all of this was to practice, practice - even when I did not feel like it.

Love has to be practiced; if you do not practice it you can never get good at it. There is a second side to this – namely, love is an *attitude of mind*. We choose to practice love or we choose not to practice love.

CHALLENGE SIX – COPING WITH UNRECIPROCATED LOVE

"How do you cope with unreciprocated love?"

This was a heartfelt question that I was asked recently. As I began to think about the question, I was drawn to another question: "Why is the love unreciprocated?"

- Is the love unreciprocated because the other person does not love you?
- Is it unreciprocated because of something that has been unforgiven?
- Is it unreciprocated because of the person that you are? For example, are you inconsistent in behaviour or manner?

It may be the first step to take is a painful and honest look at yourself. Alternatively, it may be that you have to accept that a person just does not like you or that they have fallen out of love or favour with you. This does not mean that you have done something wrong or have been at fault; it is something that you cannot control.

What you *can* control is your reaction. You are not a victim; you are a special person. You are someone who seeks to find what you can learn from a situation and how you can change, if change is needed. You have confidence in who you are, and you seek out those who love you, can help you and support you.

CHALLENGE SEVEN – LOVE IN DISAGREEMENTS

Whoever we are, there will be times when we disagree and argue. This can seem even more intense when it is with someone that we love. The positive side to this is that coming through an argument can actually strengthen a relationship.

Overcoming conflicts of this nature become easier if we remember five important points:

1. That we love this person standing before us
2. That the person that we love is a mirror of our words and actions
3. That we will never find fault or harshly reprimand
4. That forgiveness will always be sought and offered
5. That the sun will never go down on our anger (Ephesians 4:26)

Take a moment to reflect on what happens in a disagreement or argument where anger is allowed to creep in. A dark veil descends. Dear friend, what is dark is not of God. Our attraction toward the other person diminishes or disappears. We highlight and begin to exaggerate the bad points in the other person and, in extreme cases, we can even in that moment wish and voice harm upon them.

We may begin to use words such as "you always" or "you never". Things from the past may begin to well up and we become aggressive, raising our voices in order to dominate the other person, gaining a sort of satisfaction if they break down, cry or become timid.

This may seem a shocking thought: if the opposite to love is hate (and the actions in this scenario are certainly opposite to loving ones) then we have reached the door of hate, albeit for a brief period of time.

Why do I use the word 'hate'? Let's take a look at what the word hate means. The definition of hate is 'to detest and feel hostility or animosity toward a person or thing'. Reaching this point in an argument is totally destructive and also physiologically harmful as it releases all manner of chemicals that upset the normal flow, particularly if sustained through unforgiveness.

The challenge here is to put into practice the steps that we have already discussed. It is also important to think about what angers you, particularly what angers you in your relationships, and to deal with those issues before an argument arises.

The beliefs that we hold, the way in which we think, and the type of language that we use can all be adjusted so that our self-esteem is raised and we do not see ourselves as a victim.

What we practise will eventually become the norm for us so that under pressure we will natural act as we have conditioned ourselves, removing the negative context of words such as:

- "It's not fair."
- "You always..."
- "You never..."
- "You must... / mustn't..."
- "You should... / shouldn't..."

Take time to picture yourself in an argument and recall what it was like and how you felt. Now picture yourself in the same scenario but this time you are calm and confident, listening to the other person and giving your points across calmly. Bring back the first picture - see it, feel it and then make it small and dark. Flash back the picture in which you are calm and confident; make it large and bright; see it and feel it. Repeat this process until you just see that good image.

CHALLENGE EIGHT – TEARS OF LOVE, COMPASSION AND JOY

There are times when love is so great and intense that tears of love and compassion flood out. We cannot stop this emotion. I am not ashamed to admit tears when I have seen someone I really cared about walking away and choosing a destiny that they know is not going to bring ultimate happiness but meets a short term desire. There are also times when I have come across people on television with healing needs unmet, as well as people upset by the deep hurts inflicted needlessly upon them by the thoughtlessness of others. This is nothing compared with the tears and compassion of Jesus. Twice in the Bible we read that Jesus wept. At the death of His friend Lazarus we read:

John 11:33, 35

He was deeply moved in spirit and was troubled ... Jesus wept.

The other occasion was over an entire city of people:

Luke 19:41, 42

And when He approached, He saw the city and wept over it saying, if you had known in this day, even you, the things which make for peace! But now they have been hidden from your eyes.

In these examples we see a love that reduces Jesus to tears. On the one hand it is for a dear friend and on the other it is for an entire city where Jesus, just as Nehemiah (Nehemiah 1:4) and Jeremiah (Jeremiah 4:19) had done before him, wept over the city. They were all expressing extreme pain and anguish, a love so deep that it literally hurt and broke their hearts at what they saw. This is a point and depth of love that perhaps many of us do not reach. We are not so moved by what we see happening in our churches and all around us, where God's word and power have been so diluted that it is almost impossible to distinguish between the world and the church, where believers are deceived into compromising in order to increase membership or fearful of upsetting people through the word of God. We ask, "Where have the miracles and power of God gone? Where is the love of God?" The Psalmist offers to us these answers:

Psalm 34:18, 19

The Lord is near to the broken-hearted, and saves the crushed in spirit. Many are the afflictions of the righteous; but the Lord delivers him out of them all.

Psalm 51:17

The sacrifice acceptable to God is a broken spirit; a broken and contrite heart, O God, thou wilt not despise.

To see the mighty moving power of God at work that touches those who come into contact with it requires brokenness in heart and spirit. Take a moment to ponder and reflect upon the words recorded by Isaiah:

Isaiah 57: 15

I dwell in the high and holy place, and also with him who is of a contrite and humble spirit, to revive the spirit of the humble, and to revive the heart of the contrite.

Here we find an amazing, positive and uncomplicated statement: God dwells with those who have a contrite and humble heart. God searches the minds and hearts of all men and it is from what God finds that determines what we are able to show and give to others. How can I say this?

Jeremiah 17: 10

I the Lord search the mind and try the heart, to give to every man according to his ways, according to the fruit of his doings.

If we are to walk in the presence and power of God, we must first reach a point of brokenness and love at which we will receive strength through the joy of the Lord (Nehemiah 8:10).

The compassion of Jesus is also expressed when He meets people in distress and in need of healing:

Matthew 9:36

And seeing the multitudes, He felt compassion for them because they were distressed and downcast like sheep without a shepherd.

Matthew 20:34

And moved with compassion, Jesus touched their eyes; and immediately they regained their sight and followed Him.

Luke 7:13

And when the Lord saw her, He felt compassion for her and said to her, 'Do not weep.'

Tears of Joy are those that well up from within us when something good happens to those whom we love. If we take up the challenge and grow in love and compassion our tears may well increase.

Meditating on Love

By using the term 'meditation' I am talking about taking time to relax and becoming aware of the purpose for which you are seeking to meditate.

The Latin root for meditation is the word *mederi* which means 'to heal'; meditation is therefore a process of reflecting our minds upon something in order to heal it. Those things that we think about, we believe and act in line with; therefore meditation should always be upon those things that are positive and bring goodness and wholeness.

I am nothing without love and everything with it. There is no safer and better place to go than to meditate upon the words of the Bible, and so there you will find words of love and healing.

1 John 3:18
Let us not love with words or tongue but with actions and in truth.

1 John 4:18
There is no fear in love; but perfect love casts out fear...

1 Peter 4:8,9
Above all, love each other deeply, because love covers over a multitude of sins. Offer hospitality to one another without grumbling.

1 Corinthians 13:7,8
Love bears all things, believes all things, hopes all things, and endures all things. Love never ends.

John 13:34
A new commandment I give to you, that you love one another; as I have loved you, that you also love one another.

Song of Solomon 8:7
Many waters cannot quench love, neither can floods drown it.

Ephesians 5:2
Walk in love, as Christ loved us and gave Himself up for us.

John 15:13

Greater love has no man than this, that a man lay down his life for his friends.

I Corinthians 14:1

Make love your aim.

1 John 2:5

Whoever keeps His word, in him truly love for God is perfected.

Love is activated in our lives by and through the Word of God put into action.

A PROMISE

Hebrews 13:5

I will never fail you or forsake you.

THE TREASURE OF LOVE:

Matthew 6:21

For where your treasure is, there your heart will be also.

LOVE - A FRUIT OF THE SPIRIT

Galatians 5:22

But the fruit of the Spirit is love, joy, peace, longsuffering, kindness, goodness, faithfulness, gentleness, and self-control.

Love is not only described here as a fruit of the Holy Spirit but is also (not by accident or 'luck of the draw') the first to be mentioned of the nine fruits. If you want to know whether a person is walking closely with God and in the Holy Spirit, look for these fruits in their lives. If love is not oozing from our very being then we are not walking in the Spirit and close to God.

We have discovered in this chapter how important love is. God is love, Jesus demonstrated love, we are called to love God, we are called to love one another (even our enemies) and, of course, we should love ourselves.

Love is an outwardly seen indicator of our sanctification, our holiness, and our walk with God. Love crosses all boundaries and it unites all people. We do not need to speak the same mother tongue for love oozes from our very being. If love is not evident in the Christian's countenance, how can others see the fruit of the Holy Spirit and God in them?

We need to walk by the Spirit, seek the Holy Spirit's stirring and release these fruits from our lives. This is a daily journey from which we will never look back, one of holiness and power that few walk deeply in.

Many of us need to rekindle the childlike simplicity of love, faith and trust that has been damaged through growing up and been knocked back by life's experiences. It is not love that has changed; *we* have changed. This is not necessarily through our own fault, but we can rediscover ourselves. Love is not about weakness; it is about strength, healing, hope, belief and faith.

Love requires that we set aside 'self' and selfish desires and become one with God, walking in His footsteps. In Ephesians 5:1,2 we are told to imitate God and walk in love so that (1 Corinthians 16:14) all that we do is done in love.

At the beginning of this chapter, I asked the question, "What is love?" We read in 1 John 4:8, "God is love." If we know God, and walk with Him and in His ways, we will know and walk in love.

The question is, "Do we really know God?" In the same way that we get to know a person because we share with them and spend time with them, the only way to know God is to know our sin and gift of salvation.

Spend time in God's Word and talk with Him in prayer. It is only after we have done this that we can really, truly and deeply know and appreciate the love that God has for us.

1 John 4: 19
We love because He first loved us.

Knowing and living in that love is a most wonderful place to be.

Come now before God. Reach out and accept His love. Ask Him to bless you, to meet your need and to flow within every aspect of your being.

2. The Language of Forgiveness

Luke 23:34
And Jesus said, 'Father, forgive them; for they know not what they do.'

Introduction

History reveals that the whole notion of mercy and forgiveness are attributes that were not particularly foremost in the mind and lives of the ancient world. The arrival of Jesus and the emphasis of the New Testament changed all of this. What Jesus did throughout his life, and so dramatically in and through his death, was to highlight the open channel of forgiveness of sins and a new way of life through reconciliation and holy living. Jesus opened the door that reveals the true heart and nature of God and, as we see from the words of Jesus quoted at the start of this chapter, despite terrible persecution, pain and rejection Jesus was able to say, "Forgive them."

What an amazing scene! Whilst hanging on the cross in excruciating pain and being mercilessly derided, Jesus selflessly demonstrated and proclaimed ultimate love by laying down his life for us - that is, for you and me. In this single act he granted to us forgiveness for what we have done as a result of our sinful nature. Put simply, he willingly laid down his life so that we might have life or, as we read in the first letter of John:

1 John 3:16
By this we know love, that he laid down his life for us.

Why was Jesus doing this for us? The words of the parallel scripture from the gospel of John explain:

John 3:16
For God so loved the world that He gave his only son, that whoever believes in him should not perish but have eternal life.

In both this verse and in Ephesians 4:32 (where we read the words "be kind to one another, tender hearted, forgiving one another, as God in

Christ forgave you") we discover that the originator of forgiveness is God. Yes, that literally means that it is God who made the first move by reaching out to us; the means by which this was conveyed and made possible was through His only son, Jesus.

In the same way, Christian believers are to respond first to those sins and transgressions perpetrated against them. Expressed through these actions the central message of Christianity is articulated: we, each one of us, are in need of forgiveness of our sins and Jesus, through his personal sacrifice, has met that need. Put simply, if there is no forgiveness there is no Christian faith, and if there is no Christian faith there is no means of reaching the kingdom of God.

Forgiveness lies at the very heart of God, and the Christian follower is also to reflect God's love and what He has done for us by living a life of forgiveness - that is, to both forgive and be forgiven. This message is one of the central tenets of the Lord's Prayer. Jesus, responding to a request from one of his disciples to be taught how to pray, said:

Luke 11:2-4

When you pray, say: 'Father, hallowed be thy name. Thy kingdom come. Give us each day our daily bread; and forgive us our sins, for we ourselves forgive every one who is indebted to us, and lead us not into temptation.

On another occasion we come across Jesus teaching his disciples about the power of faith and, as part of this lesson on having faith in God, Jesus concludes by saying:

Mark 11:24,25

Therefore I tell you, whatever you ask in prayer, believe that you have received it, and it will be yours. And whenever you stand praying, forgive, if you have anything against any one; so that your Father also who is in heaven may forgive you your trespasses.

Forgiveness is not only an important message in the Christian faith; it is also an active and proactive response that God requires and expects from us. Why do I say this? Take a look at what Jesus said:

John 15:12
This is my commandment, that you love one another as I have loved you.

And yet the question remains: are we in obedience to this commandment?

It has been claimed that the American Baptist minister and Bible scholar Clarence Jordan (1912 – 1969) once said, "We'll worship the hind legs off Jesus, then not lift a finger to do a single thing he says." The statement may be stark but the sentiment behind Jordan's words resonates to the depths of my soul. It is all too easy to do the things that suit us or to take a little pain and sacrifice a little of ourselves, but the exercise of our faith and love for God come through total obedience, and this is no less true in the obedience to God's word to forgive.

Obedient In Forgiveness

Forgiveness is not dependent upon conditions or circumstances. Love expressed through forgiveness does not harbour bitterness, anger, hate, resentment or revenge.

Logically, this all means that...

...demonstrating unforgiveness in our lives is a sign that we do not truly love God.

Gosh, what a powerful statement that is; but is it true? In the first letter of John we read:

1 John 4:20,21
If any one says, 'I love God', and hates his brother, he is a liar; for he who does not love his brother whom he has seen, cannot love God whom he has not seen. And this commandment we have from him, that he who loves God should love his brother also.

And again we read in the same letter of John:

1 John 2:11
He who hates his brother is in darkness and walks in the darkness, and does not know where he is going, because the darkness has blinded his eyes.

Darkness, of course, is the domain of Satan. Have you ever been in a place where there is literally no light? Some years ago, as part of an exercise of trust, I was with a group of people walking through an underground cave. All of the torches were turned off and, literally, you could not see your hand in front of your face. To all intents and purposes we were blinded by the darkness and disorientated. Hate and unforgiveness prevent us from seeing anything but the darkness of hate.

The importance of loving one another, our brothers and sisters in Christ as well as our neighbour, is highlighted so clearly in these scripture verses. Indeed if this strength of love does not flow, it hinders or grieves the Holy Spirit and the moral standing of the Christian faith is brought into disrepute. In his letter to the Ephesians Paul writes:

Ephesians 4: 26 – 32

Be angry but do not sin.

[Paul realistically recognises that we may be stirred to anger over certain issues. We all have a sense of what is right and what is wrong, what is just and what is unjust. Our sense of fairness and fair play will be aroused, producing with them strength of feelings, but Paul goes on to say...]

...do not let the sun go down on your anger, and give no opportunity to the devil. Let the thief no longer steal, but rather let him labour, doing honest work with his hands, so that he may be able to give to those in need. Let no evil talk come out of your mouths, but only such as is good for edifying, as fits the occasion, that it may impart grace to those who hear. And do not grieve the Holy Spirit of God, in whom you were sealed for the day of redemption. Let all bitterness and wrath and anger and clamour and slander be put away from you, with all malice, and be kind to one another, tender hearted, forgiving one another, as God in Christ forgave you.

Even though we ourselves are sinners acting in ways that upset God, He forgives us; so we too, recognising our own faults and the fact that we are ourselves forgiven, must do likewise. Yes, we have been hurt. Yes, it

65

may be unjust. But if we look to ourselves we too must recognise and be thankful that we are forgiven.

Forgiveness is a conscious and deliberate act of our will.

Through forgiveness we unavoidably share in Christ's sufferings, but the paradox here is that as we do this we also share in the abundance of Christ's comfort. What basis do I have to say this? Take a look at the following statement:

1 Corinthians 1:3-5
Blessed be the God and Father of our Lord Jesus Christ, the Father of mercies and God of all comfort, who comforts us in all our affliction, so that we may be able to comfort those who are in affliction, with the comfort with which we ourselves are comforted by God. For as we share abundantly in Christ's sufferings, so through Christ we share abundantly in comfort too.

Unforgiveness brings with it anger, unease, separation, resentment, illness and many more disruptive and harmful elements that Satan uses to his advantage and effect. In short, unforgiveness is sin. The only way in which these are relieved is through forgiveness. It is not about a person appearing to 'win' unfairly; it is about receiving God's comfort and peace of mind. It is about being faithful, trusting and being obedient to God. It is about receiving His blessings as we submit to Him and reveal the kingdom of God to others through our forgiving actions.

Forgiveness is about absorbing sin and reducing its impact.

Paul writes these words:

Colossians 1:24
Now I rejoice in my sufferings for your sake, and in my flesh I complete what is lacking in Christ's affliction for the sake of his holy body, that is, the church.

On first reading it looks here as if Paul is suggesting that Christ did not do enough on the cross and that he, Paul, is filling in for the missing bits that Christ left out. Has Paul placed himself 'above his station'? Has he gone mad? Is this blasphemy?

Let's take a closer look at what Paul is trying to express here. Firstly, no, Paul is not thinking higher of himself than he ought to, he has not gone mad and he is certainly not blaspheming. What Paul is saying is that Christ, through his death on the cross, has paid the ultimate price for our sin. He has taken the sting of spiritual death away for those who would believe in him and accept him as Lord and saviour, so that having done this we can enter the kingdom of heaven if we choose to do so through giving ourselves to him. It is plainly obvious that what Christ did not do on the cross was to remove sin from the world; we are still living in a sinful world and Christians will suffer just as much as anyone else from the effects of sin.

What Paul is effectively saying is that forgiveness is a means by which absorption of the effects of sin takes place. As Christians, through forgiveness we take on the painful effects of sin and stop these sins and hurts that confront us from spreading. This act of love expressed through forgiveness literally binds the damaging effects that would otherwise spread like a terrible disease.

Unforgiveness is sin and it causes strife, which keeps sin active as it bounces backwards and forwards, spiralling downward and getting increasingly worse as reaction meets further reaction. This ever-deepening, ever-worsening situation can spread and affect others. Even innocent bystanders can be affected when they meet our inner anger; it uncontrollably explodes, drawing them in as a result. Or they can be affected when we react in situations that are totally unrelated yet our reactions are the result of unforgiven hurts. The hurts snap at the heels of anything that dares to cross our paths, thereby spreading sin further afield.

The act of forgiveness sucks in the sin as it hits us instead of rebounding and causing havoc. It stops the thread of the sin, and in some cases it brings a person to conviction. How another person responds is their sole responsibility and God will deal with them in due time. We can learn to offload hurts that affect us to God through prayer and love rather than to bounce them back and make matters worse in the process.

Forgiveness Exemplified

Christians are called to be examples, just as Christ was our example, and we can also learn from one another. Let's take a look now at some people who have suffered yet maintained their faith in God and have acted in obedience to Him through forgiveness.

EXAMPLE ONE

In May of 1981 the world was shocked by the actions of assassin Mehmet Ali Agca who raised his gun and coldly shot John Paul II inflicting a near fatal wound. Reported in Time Magazine and published across the globe, John Paul II had embraced Ali Agca in his inimitable way and whispered to him words of forgiveness.

It did not stop there. John Paul II often visited his would-be-assassin and even joined the campaign to have him released from an Italian jail so that he could return to his own country.

When asked why he had forgiven Ali Agca, John Paul II replied that it is what Christ had commanded. What the Pontiff demonstrated is that Christianity is not simply about what we say and how we extol Christ; it is about putting into practice Christ-like living in our own daily lives.

As the world looks in upon the Christian church it should not see a microcosm of the world, huddled together - bold in words but fruitless in action and the demonstration of practical obedience and power of God.

EXAMPLE TWO

In 1987, whilst standing carefree and happy with his beloved daughter Marie watching a Remembrance Day service parade in Enniskillen, a terrorist's bomb detonated and Gordon Wilson, still holding his daughter's hand, was buried with her under a pile of rubble. Marie lost her life that day along with nine other bystanders.

When interviewed about the bombing that had claimed his daughter's life, Gordon Wilson's selfless act was to express his forgiveness towards those who had planted the device. He added that he would pray for them and pleaded that no one would take revenge for his daughter's death. The loss of their daughter shattered Gordon and his wife, but as Christians they were eager that this small town would not be torn apart by the tragedy and that the people would be reconciled and live in harmony with one another again, as they had previously done.

Let us not fool ourselves; it does not take much to realise from these examples amongst hundreds and thousands of others that forgiveness is not an easy act. It is not something that comes naturally, and it all so often comes amidst great pain, injustice and even sacrifice. The alternative, although it rolls off our thoughts and feelings easily as we seek 'justice' through retribution and revenge, is far more destructive and hurtful in the long run.

EXAMPLE THREE

This is the amazing story of Helen Campbell who tragically lost both her daughter Susan and granddaughter Kimberley in what can only be described as an act of horrendous and mindless disregard for life.

Two young men entered the house of Helen's daughter and granddaughter whilst they lay asleep. As they broke into the house the young men aged nineteen and twenty were met by the two family dogs which they killed. They then went upstairs and attacked young Kimberley. Hearing the commotion, her mother went to see what was happening. The attackers turned on Susan and stabbed her several times. One of the young attackers exclaimed later that he did not realise that it was so difficult to kill a person and slit Susan's throat. The attackers then turned again to Kimberley and she became unconscious; they then set the house ablaze.

When interviewed some eight years later, Helen Campbell astonishingly quoted from Psalm 119:71 which says, "It is good for me that I was afflicted, that I might learn thy statutes." She then said that she wouldn't have got close to Jesus if she had not lost her daughter and granddaughter. Obviously still deeply affected by the atrocity, Helen said that she hated what these two men had done but she did not hate them. Helen explained that she wanted God to love her and, quoting from God's words, she went on to say that it is simple - if we do not forgive others, God will not forgive us.

Helen Campbell wrote to the two men in prison saying that she forgave them for what they had done and also implored them to ask God's forgiveness. She went on to explain that she would pray that the Holy Spirit would let them know that Jesus died on the cross for them, that he loves them and that they need to believe in Jesus, ask his forgiveness and give their hearts to him.

Helen said that she believes that the Holy Spirit has directed her path. She explained that to live in unforgiveness is to cripple oneself; it prevents love and growth. She also stated that humility is the biggest act that one can take in life. It is a matter of humbling oneself before God and letting him take over. When asked what good had come out of the tragedy, she simply said, "Turning my life totally over to God."

Trusting God and obeying his command to forgive has not removed the pain of her loss, but it has lifted her out of the torment and shackles that unforgiveness otherwise offers.

The Torment of Unforgiveness

What is unforgiveness? The dictionary definitions include 'not being disposed to forgive or to show mercy' and 'not allowing for mistakes, carelessness or weakness.'

All of the time that we bear unforgiveness we place ourselves in the prison of constraint that the sinful offence against us has opened the door to. It is worth stopping and noting this point again. We, as an active response, place ourselves in the prison called unforgiveness. The offence has only opened the channel which leads to the door, but we make the conscious choice to walk into the prison through our unforgiving nature; alternatively, we can side-step the prison through forgiveness. Slipping into the channel of unforgiveness is a natural reaction to the offence, our sense of fair play and our notion of right and wrong. Entering through the prison door of unforgiveness comes when we react in retaliation, spite, anger, revenge and resentment, showing no forgiveness or mercy and making no allowances.

Unforgiveness produces a merry-go-round of venom, spite, resentment and hatred, which will never end if we do not get the unforgiveness out of our system and jump off. We can find all manner of excuses for delaying forgiveness, but these only serve to bind us up; our hope, peace, joy and healing are held back.

If we choose (and it is a choice we personally take) to enter the prison of unforgiveness then the more we entrench ourselves in our 'rights', revenge, 'justice', hate and resentment the thicker the walls of our prison become. The thicker the walls of our prison become the more we will be starved of freedom, peace and God's presence. Unforgiveness creates a separation between God and us in that it affects our prayer link and also our relationship with God. It stops the anointing and power of God in our lives. Jesus, at the end of his teaching on how to pray, put it this way:

Matthew 6:14,15

For if you forgive men their trespasses, your heavenly Father also will forgive you; but if you do not forgive men their trespasses, neither will your Father forgive your trespasses.

In its wake, unforgiveness creates a block in the flow of love. It also has a deeply profound effect upon our health and wellbeing because it disrupts the harmony of our body systems, creates a disturbance of our brain waves and creates stress and anxiety. Recent psychological and medical studies associate this anxiety with health problems similar to those of chronic stress disorders, including causing muscle tension, high blood pressure and imbalance of body cells; these can lead to serious illnesses such as heart disease, arthritis and cancer.

What we are learning here is that our choice to be unforgiving has a direct impact on our own physiological, psychological and spiritual health. It is a sobering thought that all too often unforgiveness has a costly affect on us but often none on the perpetrator, who may have moved on, or has no idea how we feel, or has died. The true losers in the process of unforgiveness are you and I as individuals - our health, spiritual growth and peace of mind are compromised. The very odd and strange thing about unforgiveness is that it is really a highly effective and destructive form of self-punishment.

We will all know from even our comparatively minor experiences of 'a trespass against us' that forgiveness is not an easy step to take, and yet it is a commandment of God that many fall into disobedience over. Is God being unreasonable in His demand that even goes as far as to say that He will not forgive us if we fail to forgive others?

God never said that becoming a Christian would be an easy way of life, but it is a blessed and fulfilled way of life. When we realise just how destructive unforgiveness is and how it cuts us off from God we actually realise that God is not being unreasonable in His expectation at all. In fact, there is no real choice to make other than to take the path of forgiveness. Forgiveness is the wise choice and it brings us closer to God.

The Law of Forgiveness

On thinking about the question of forgiveness, the Apostle Peter went to Jesus and asked, "Lord, how often shall my brother sin against me, and I forgive him? As many as seven times?" Jesus said to him, "I do not say to you seven times, but seventy times seven" (Matthew 18:21,22).

Peter is clearly aware that forgiveness is necessary, but he asks how often a person who repeats their transgression should be forgiven. By offering a number to his own question, Peter is wondering if there is a limit to grace. The response of Jesus is effectively that there is no limit.

Jesus then goes on by teaching why forgiveness is so necessary through a parable (Matthew 18:23-35). Here a servant is in debt, owing a large sum of money, so he is about to be sold along with his wife, children and possessions. The servant begs his master for time to pay back what he owes. Out of mercy the master releases the servant from punishment. When this servant has left his master he comes across a fellow servant who owes him a fraction of the debt that he has been released from. Even though this fellow servant pleads for time to pay, the request is met with a firm refusal and he is put in prison. On hearing about this incident the master places the unforgiving servant in prison.

The fact is, as a Christian we have been forgiven a huge debt.

Romans 6:23:

For the wages of sin is death, but the free gift of God is eternal life in Christ Jesus our Lord.

Because we have been forgiven the price of a huge debt it is our obligation to forgive trespasses against us.

Dear friend, forgiveness cannot change the past. The pain from past events, especially the loss of a loved one, will always be there, but we will never move forward unless we humble ourselves and forgive. Forgiveness can change the future.

Walking in Humility

In Micah, we come across some special words that were specifically directed at those who walk in an active and vibrant relationship with God, setting aside an empty and hypocritical faith:

Micah 6:8
He has showed you, O man, what is good; and what does the Lord require of you but to do justice, and to love kindness, and to walk humbly with your God.

The act of humbling ourselves before God removes emptiness and hypocrisy from the Christian faith and puts God in central place. We come across this same call to humility in the first letter of Peter:

1 Peter 5:5-7
Clothe yourselves, all of you, with humility toward one another, for God opposes the proud, but gives grace to the humble. Humble yourselves therefore under the mighty hand of God, that in due time he may exalt you. Cast all your anxieties on him, for he cares about you.

The call here is put off self-importance, pride and arrogance and to place ourselves totally under God's authority, to serve, to be unpretentious, to be conscious of our own failings, to recognise our place and to allow God to take control of our lives.

The Christian walk is one of paradox. Jesus taught that...

- ...if you lose your life, you will gain it – Mark 8:35
- ...if you are last, you will be first – Matthew 20:16
- ...if you are humble, you will be exalted – Luke 14:11

Humility is not about weakness and being trodden under foot. Humility is about knowing one's strengths and acknowledging one's weaknesses. Humble people will not promote themselves for gain but rather use their strengths to serve others. The proud overestimate their strengths and deny their weaknesses. They laud themselves over others, seeing themselves better than they really are. The humble person knows that God is Lord and that power and strength come only from Him. The proud person goes their own way thinking that success is born from their power and gift alone.

There is no cause for fear or concern in offering ourselves to God in humility. God will not reject us or humiliate us. As we willingly sacrifice 'self' in order to be broken and come in repentance to God, He will accept us.

James 4:10

Humble yourselves before the Lord and he will exalt you.

If we are not prepared to humble ourselves before God we will never see the fulness of mighty moves of the Holy Spirit, signs, wonders and miracles. These things can only be entrusted to those who know their place, who do as God asks and do not end up thinking of themselves more highly than they ought.

In 1896, during a revival in his Methodist church, Judson W Van De Venter (1855 – 1939) was convicted by the Holy Spirit to give up his artist teaching and to become an evangelist. Although initially resisting the call, Judson was convicted by the words of Luke 14:33 which says, "Whoever of you does not renounce all that he has cannot be my disciple." He surrendered his life to God and was inspired to write the words of the hymn 'I Surrender All'.

All to Jesus I surrender,
All to Him I freely give;
I will ever love and trust Him,
In His presence daily live.

A message that is often not proclaimed is that if we do not surrender and renounce all we cannot be a true disciple of Jesus. There is a cost to be counted in following Jesus. Paul puts it this way:

Philippians 3:7

Whatever gain I had, I counted as loss for the sake of Christ.

3. The Language of Faith

You see things; and you say, "Why?" But I dream things that never were; and I say, "Why not?"

- George Bernard Shaw -

Introduction

Godly love and the expression of this love through forgiveness open a channel for us as Christian believers to confidently and freely exercise faith in demonstration of the presence and power of God. That is why in scripture verses such as Mark 11:22-25 we see the combination of having faith in God, exercising this faith through prayer requests, clearing hindrances through forgiveness, and exercising faith in love.

In this chapter we focus our attention on the type of language that we use concerning faith, what we think and say about faith, and how where our faith is rooted it affects the way in which our beliefs, thoughts, words and actions make us who we are and what we are.

When I first began to write about faith, I came to realize the importance of the task and the great responsibility it entails. Therefore I do not take this task lightly. There are so many potential pitfalls in terms of where a person's faith is rooted. These are often further affected by the many misguided teachings regarding what faith actually is. Unfortunately it is the case that all too many of the teachings on faith are based upon interpretations of individuals rather than those of the Bible. These man-inspired teachings are not only broad but also skewed as a result of basic misunderstandings - often unintentional - emanating from a genuine personal desire to find an explanation for something that men and women have found difficult to comprehend. In the process of unbelief many have failed to walk in the Spirit, seeking clarity from God through His word; the end result causes the balance of comprehension to tip away from what is actually true.

Satan knows all too well that if Christians lock into the fulness of faith, the power of God will be unleashed in ways that have rarely been demonstrated other than in the lives of such people as Smith Wigglesworth and William Branham. The fact is that Jesus stated clearly:

John 14:12

Truly, truly [In other words, 'I am telling you the truth'], I say to you, he who believes [some versions say, 'he who has faith'] in me will also do the works that I do; and greater works than these will he do.

What this incredible statement by Jesus means is that we all - every one of us in the body of Christ - not only have the potential to demonstrate signs, wonders and miracles as a normal everyday part of our lives but to demonstrate these in ways that Jesus did not do in his limited ministry time. The problem has been that we do not actually believe this. We marvel at those who demonstrate gifts but we do not grasp the fact that this potential is at our own fingertips and available to any Christian believer. We have not grasped the fact that the reason why the words of Jesus are not more frequently manifested is a result of us not taking personal responsibility for it to happen.

The Christian church needs to address that, with a few exceptions, it has lost its power to be the effective force that God, the ministry and blood of Christ and the Holy Spirit intend. Dear friends, I say this out of a deep love and desire to take more from God than we have taken before. It is surely long overdue that we, the church, awake from our timid slumber and mediocrity; stop making incredible claims from the Bible that are not actually tangibly demonstrated in power, signs and miracles; and convert what we say into what we do. It is simply not enough to see the occasional move of God and to be satisfied; to do this is to deny the fulness of what God has promised and to walk in unbelief.

I am not trying to 'bash' the Christian church on the head just for the sake of being controversial. I am trying to honestly take a step back and reconcile where the church stands measured against what the Bible has to say about the exercise and application of faith. There are many excuses that Christians make. Some say, "We are not perfect," and yet we are *working toward* it. Some are actually quite comfortable with where they are or they make excuses that simply do not match what the Bible has to say.

I recently met a man who was tending a grave. We got talking and the man said that he had sadly lost his wife to cancer. He explained to me that the church had been wonderful to both his wife during her long illness, and also to him, and he felt supported by the love of those in the congregation. I was deeply touched by this story and challenged concerning the love that this man had received but saddened to hear that this dear lady had died in the prime of her life. The man then said something to me that shook me to the core. He said that this church was how a church should be - not in a "God squad" type of way but in caring. What became evident was that the church is a lovely, comfortable, loving place to be (and I praise God for that), but it does not want to be challenged and it lacks power. I do not personally know the church concerned and cannot make any comment about the teaching, but it left me wondering how the application of faith would have impacted.

At about the same time as the graveyard meeting I was reading a story from the ministry of Smith Wigglesworth. He had been called out to minister healing to a dying person so Smith took with him a "man of prayer". When they reached the dying person, Smith asked the man of prayer to intercede with God for the person. The prayers went along the lines of asking God to bless and support the family, to allow this person not to suffer, to have pain taken away and to die with dignity. Smith had to stop the man from praying and asked him to leave because these prayers were not prayers of faith. Smith came before God in faith and the dying man was healed. You see, it is not God's will that sickness resides in the body of anyone. Yet if you listen to the conversation and prayers of many Christians you would think that this was not the case. Where in the Bible does it say that God will not respond to faith and heal the sick?

How often are our prayers demonstrations of our lack of faith in God? What would happen if we truly had faith in God and prayed differently?

Called To Walk In Faith

During the course of writing about general shortcomings of faith in the church it occurred to me that change has not and will not happen so long as leaders and the Christian community as a whole remain locked in the same position, with the same thinking, teaching and speech that currently exist. If we continually do things that do not work then we will continually get the same result.

I am reminded of the many thousands of lives that were needlessly lost during the First World War with wave after wave of men being killed in a hail of bullets as they were ordered 'over the top'. As we look back at what intelligent officers were doing we may well be staggered by their 'blindness' in sending thousands to a certain death and for little or no gain. Surely someone must have said, "This is not working; let's look for inspiration elsewhere"? With hindsight it is easy to criticise what took place, but the point is - amazing as it may seem - we are all prone, in one way or another, to 'blindness' in our habits. In the church this occurs through traditions and teachings of men. These create a major block to God's intended purpose and perfect will because they are not from God and they blind men from the truth.

In Mark 7:1-8 Jesus rebuked the Pharisees for their hypocrisy in placing tradition above God's word, and quoting from Isaiah 29:13 he said:

Mark 7:6-8

'This people honours me with their lips, but their heart is far from me; in vain do they worship me, teaching as doctrines the precepts of men.' You leave the commandments of God, and hold fast the tradition of men.

Why do I say all of this? The truth of the matter is that...

Hebrews 11:6

Without faith it is impossible to please [God].

In other words, if we do not use our faith and apply it according to the scriptures then we are not living as God intends; we are not walking with God as He expects that we should.

We have been given Bible verses such as the following:

Matthew 7: 7

Ask, and it will be given you; seek, and you will find; knock, and it will be opened to you.

Mark 11: 24

Therefore I tell you, whatever you ask in prayer, believe that you have received it, and it will be yours.

John 14: 13

Whatever you ask in my name, I will do it, that the Father may be glorified in the Son; if you ask anything in my name, I will do it.

James 5: 15

The prayer of faith will save the sick man, and the Lord will raise him up.

Let's be completely honest. Our experience suggests that these scripture words and promises more often than not fail to be realised; as a result many seek answers by making excuses for God, interpreting what these verses say in a way that fits and satisfies them, explaining away the truth by side stepping faith issues. We overtly or covertly blame God or make the excuse that 'it was not His will'. The bottom line, dear friend, is that the Bible is not a lie. It is not God at fault here; rather we must look to ourselves. How many times do we honestly 'exercise faith' but in reality leave God out? How often do we seek to shift responsibility anywhere but onto ourselves? How often have we earnestly prayed in faith and, if an answer has not been forthcoming, gone back to God and asked Him where we are going wrong? The fact is, if the Bible says it then it must be so. This means that the weakness in the chain lies in us as individuals, and we need to look to ourselves and redress the balance. The responsibility lies with you and me. Some people reading these words may be agitated by them, but whatever our own personal reactions are, let's stop and look into God's mirror and be honest with ourselves.

The disciples were with Jesus, they were taught by him, they lived with him and they saw the miracles and healings, signs and wonders that he performed, and yet Jesus exclaims, "O you of little faith."

Matthew 6:30

But if God so clothes the grass of the field, which today is alive and tomorrow is thrown into the oven, will he not much more clothe you, O you of little faith?

Matthew 8: 26

And he said to them, 'Why are you afraid, O men of little faith?'

Matthew 14: 31

Jesus immediately reached out his hand and caught him, saying to him, 'O man of little faith, why did you doubt?'

Matthew 16:8

But Jesus, aware of this, said, 'O men of little faith, why do you discuss among yourselves the fact that you have no bread?'

Following an inability to cast out a demon in a boy, to their credit the disciples came to Jesus and asked, "Why could we not cast it out?" He replied to them:

Matthew 17:19-20

Because of your little faith. For truly, I say to you, if you have faith as a grain of mustard seed, you will say to this mountain, 'Move from here to there', and it will move; and nothing will be impossible to you.

It does not take great faith to heal the sick, see miracles, signs and wonders. It is about taking from God His promises and speaking words of command, trusting God. God offers us through Jesus the gift of faith - to exercise it with confidence in the name of Jesus.

A church where sickness remains within its members, or where people die from disease and illness, is a church that is powerless and demonstrating 'little faith'. The question is, why in the Christian church do we not see the fulness of God's power? Why are signs, wonders, miracles and healings lacking? Is the answer found in Matthew 13:58 and Mark 6:6?

Matthew 13:58

And he did not do many mighty works there, because of their unbelief.

Mark 6: 6

And he marvelled because of their unbelief.

Jesus was astounded by the fact that people were either unwilling or unable to exercise faith in demonstration of power. Faith has to be used. The more it is used, the more it will develop and the more confidence we have in God, as it moves from our head understanding to heart understanding. Whilst ministering to the sick and needy Jesus himself said:

Matthew 9:29

According to your faith be it done to you.

What we witness in the church is according to the faith exercised within it.

In one form or another there are many places in the Bible where we are told to have faith in God, but what does this mean? It means 'trust God for who He is and what He is; trust Him to do exactly what He says He will do'. We have conditioned ourselves to think that God will not act, but in our weakness we can call out to God and trust Him to act on His promises.

In Isaiah 6:1-13 we read how Isaiah was confronted by the holiness of God; his response was to immediately repent, confess his failings and seek cleansing. God called saying, "Whom shall I send, and who will go for us?" (Isaiah 6:8). The response of Isaiah was, "Here am I. Send me."

Release of faith and demonstration of God's power in the church starts with us as individuals. We need to repent, confess our past failings and respond to the call of God to walk in faith.

Test the Word Of God

Our guide is the Bible, the Word of God, and it is truth. I have said this already, but I will say it again: if what is being said by someone is not in the Bible or it contradicts what the Bible has to say then do not allow these thoughts to pollute and settle in your mind.

What I am about to say may seem very odd when talking about faith. However, I hope that readers of these words will appreciate the sincerity and depth of responsibility that I feel when I say that it is very important to maintain rationality, use common sense and check all things. Faith is not about launching headlong into something 'willy-nilly' or going around metaphorically blindfolded.

It is so easy to believe what we hear and read without testing its validity. As a child I was told that I would 'never be any good'. Indeed, I failed in some things and so what I had been told was true. I had the evidence - or did I? I ended up carrying that false stigma and belief for most of my life. For many people reading this it may come as a surprise, especially to those that are sceptics, that even the Bible, in several different places, encourages us to test what we hear, read and see. For example:

1 Thessalonians 5:21
Test all things, hold fast what is good.

We all have, albeit in various measures, the attribute known as 'common sense' - the ability to know what is right and what is wrong, to apply reason and logic, to test situations and ask questions - and it is important to apply this in appropriate measure.

Let me explain a little further. It is easy to listen to, or read, something from a great teacher or leader and to be convinced by what they are saying, especially in emotion-packed gatherings or emotional states of mind. It is quite natural for our enquiring minds to seek answers or to deflect blame from ourselves. We cannot underestimate the power of words, especially the power of the words that we allow to enter our inner thoughts and daily language, because what we think will affect our beliefs, behaviours and actions. This is why it is so important to flood our minds with the Word of God.

The words and type of language that we use have a cause and effect. What we say and think are linked closely with our physiology, behaviour and the actions that we subsequently take. In order to provide an example to illustrate this point, try the following experiment with a partner:

Stand with your arm raised out in front of you. Now ask your partner to apply a downward pressure on top of your arm, just above the elbow. Notice what happens.

Lower your arm, give it a gentle shake and then raise it again as before. This time think about words such as tired, weak, lethargic, unable, downtrodden and unhappy. Try and picture these states in your mind. After a short while your partner applies a downward pressure on top of your arm, just above the elbow. Notice what happens.

Again, lower your arm, give it a gentle shake and raise it again as before. This time think about words such as alive, strong, powerful, able, upright and happy. Picture these and again after a short while your partner applies a downward pressure.

Notice how the words that you used and thought about affected the way you felt and reacted.

Although there is some disagreement regarding the percentage of human nonverbal communication, it is said that between 60 - 90% of our communication is through body language. In other words, a person's body language is generally an indicator of their state of mind and attitude. Those who are seasoned performers know that the power of their words mixed with emotional settings and the way in which they hold their body, where they look and the strength that they show through their body all impact on how they are received by the listener. No matter how compelling these people may seem, the Bible must be our reference, guide and teacher.

I know from a lifetime of involvement in sport, just as any spectator will also observe, how the body language of a losing or defeated athlete with slumped shoulders and head hanging down is so different from that of the victor who can be seen leaping and punching the air. Even more incredible is that despite the seeming odds building up against some athletes who go through a 'down' period during the course of their performance, they are able to muster a call upon their inner resources. We see and even hear them talking to themselves, speaking words of encouragement. Sometimes they are able to look at (or take time out to speak with) their coach, and suddenly the spectator is able to see a total change in body language as the athlete gains in confidence and fights their way through to victory from a seeming position of defeat. Why? Because they believed (and had faith in this belief) that they could overcome, and they started to call upon positive thoughts and speak with positive language. The power resource of faith is immense. The difference between winning and losing, between champions and world champions, is what goes on between their ears - what they think, say and do.

How often have we seen exhausted competitors sag to their knees after a gruelling event? And yet the winner, though equally exhausted, is able to summon an inner strength that comes from their pride, joy and elation of winning. In these examples we have a clear indication of just how powerful our mindset can be and how interlinked it is with our physiology.

It is not only necessary but also a natural part of human nature to have beliefs and faith. Being able to place our faith in someone or something heightens our ability to succeed. Where we place our beliefs and faith, and the accuracy and reliability of these, are ours to test, examine and determine. This is an ongoing process so that we can re-evaluate what I have called the 'world is flat' syndrome; faith is an active process of 'learning more about it', 'applying it' and 'celebrating in it'.

There are degrees and levels of faith. These lead us to distinguish between lacking in faith, having little faith, having faith and possessing great faith. As a result of experiences faith can be temporarily (or at best permanently) heightened, allowing people to accomplish great things and overcome great odds.

Following on from our sports example another important aspect to the cause and effect of language relates to how we interpret the words that are used. The impact upon us of words such as "I hate you", "I resent you" or "I love you", "I forgive you" can be far-reaching. Of course, the emphasis and tone placed on the words that we speak heighten or lessen the impact. It makes sense then that we use and project our words carefully and that we check what certain words actually mean. In doing so we can benefit from the richness of all that lies behind the things we say, and we can steer our speech away from negativity and destruction, to bring positivity and creativity - not only to ourselves but also to others. If our speech is not positive it is better to be silent. Why not try it and see the results for yourself?

This leads us to a further aspect of the words that we use:

Ephesians 4:29

Let no corrupt communication [some translations say 'evil talk'] proceed out of your mouth, but what is good for necessary edification, that it may impart grace to the hearers.

The word 'corrupt' is interesting here because it means more than the use of bad language which 'evil talk' may imply. We find that it can also mean:

- 'To make meaningless or different in meaning by scribal errors or alterations.'
- 'To infect and contaminate.'
- 'To alter from the original.'

Now this throws a different light on the impact of the words that we use. How can we edify and impart grace if we are not speaking God's actual word?

If you want to check how effective your communication with another person is, how good their communication with you is, or even how effective your own internal communication is, take time to look at the responses that you get. Did your words or thoughts have the desired effect? If you are unsure about the meaning behind what someone has said, repeat it back to them or, if unable to do this, check the information and work on the basis that the meaning of communication is the response.

Where, in whom, and how we apply our faith and talk about it will (as with any other form of language that we use) have a direct affect upon what we believe, how we act, and what outcomes are achieved in our lives.

Integrity

Before I launch further into this topic, in maintaining my integrity regarding writing about faith, it is important that readers of this understand that I have grappled with faith issues for a number of years. This work is a combination of my personal search; research and experience in sport and sport psychology; my reading of the Bible; the work of Smith Wigglesworth, William Branham and many others; along with my own prayer that God would enlighten me. I am sharing here my thoughts with a view not to claim any special knowledge but rather to humbly stimulate readers to take a fresh look at what faith really means and how faith language can have a positive effect. I am also mindful that it is insufficient to *talk* about faith; it is something that should be a part of my daily walk. I am, in honesty, working on this and recognise my many weaknesses. I cannot even hold a candle to some of the great faith exponents and practitioners. I am also mindful that it is not my place to compare myself with others but rather to trust God and be a person of faith.

Due to its importance, I make no apology for repeating several times during the course of this book that no matter what perspective you approach faith from there can be no substitute for readers carrying out their own research on this topic and checking for themselves the legitimacy of what the word 'faith' actually means and how in turn this may affect their lives. It is a personal journey that carries with it a personal responsibility to trust.

At this point I would have liked to illustrate what I have been saying about faith by using an example from someone. I have found however that this is insufficient, as those who demonstrate faith in turn focus themselves in one direction - namely the source of proven support, inspiration and reliability. We could of course talk about how soldiers on the battlefield can have faith in the support that they have one for another, or how firefighters can work in the faith that others in the team will work as one unit or even how we can have faith that friends or loved ones will put their lives at risk to save ours. However, any example used will point us to the source of inspiration:

Hebrews 12:2

...fixing our eyes [or looking] on Jesus, the author and perfecter of faith.

Here we find that the biblical inspiration and perfection of faith is personified. If we want to know how to exercise faith then we can begin by looking at Jesus.

The language of this message is very clear: faith is the only way to, as Smith Wigglesworth once put it, "unlock the treasures of God". If faith is that important then it is crucial to understand what faith is. The importance placed upon faith in attaining success, and particularly with regard to the biblical definition, cannot be overstated. However it is equally important that a misunderstanding of what faith actually is must be avoided because it can lead to confusion and difficulties.

I read recently of an account where someone quoted from the Bible, saying that "God will provide all of your needs" (Philippians 4:19). Instead of stopping to understand the context and meaning, this was interpreted as a promised that the person concerned did not have to pay their debts because God would meet that need as they put their faith in Him. This example demonstrates a lack of understanding regarding what faith actually is and how to apply it. Therefore let us take some time to understand faith.

What Faith Is Not

In order to dispel some misconceptions about faith it is important to understand that I am not talking here about faith being a particular religion. When talking about a person's 'religious faith' the word usually refers to the doctrines, traditions, beliefs and methods used within that particular religion. Faith in our context here is certainly not about any one religion or general religious belief and stance.

The faith that I am talking about is also not about manipulation or manoeuvring a situation to suit a particular outcome that we may want. It is not about trying to place God in a position that suits our need so that we can shift our responsibility and actions onto God or even blame God if we do not get what we want. It is also not about finding our own explanations to fit what we want to believe.

Faith is not an intellectual acknowledgement where on the one hand we agree with what the Bible says whilst on the other hand our understanding has no life-changing effect. It is also not about accepting the parts that we want to accept whilst placing into a cupboard anything that we do not want to accept or find difficult to understand.

Faith is not about desire, positive thinking, hoping or waiting for results. It is also not wishful thinking.

A number of mistakes have been made concerning what the word 'faith' actually means, and much of this is sadly based upon mistaken teaching, particularly in churches and schools, so that we now have terms such as taking a 'leap of faith' or 'blind faith'. Faith was never intended to be a leap or to be blind.

'Leap of Faith' and 'Blind Faith'

The term 'leap of faith' is a corrupted attribution to the writings of the Danish philosopher and theologian Soren Aabye Kierkegaard (1813 – 1855). I say corrupted because actually he never used the term 'leap of faith' but rather 'leap *to* faith'. Many, including C.S. Lewis, have been critical of the term 'leap of faith' and argue that there is logic and evidential support for biblical faith. Jesus referred to the miracles that he did as being evidence of who he said he was.

John 14.11
Believe me that I am in the Father and the Father in me; or else believe me for the sake of the works themselves.

Capturing the essence of the terms 'leap of faith' and 'blind faith' Mark Twain is quoted as saying, "Faith is believing what you know ain't so."

Each of these examples effectively suggests that faith is about walking in the dark, having no examples or evidence upon which to build. This position is really more about the 'blind leading the blind', where one is in danger of accepting whatever new fad or idea may come their way or whatever convicting speaker or leader may say without testing the truth and legitimacy of the teaching. Faith must be accompanied by some form of evidence; otherwise it is 'blind'. Again we learn from the Bible that the source and nourishment of faith comes from hearing about it from the evidence of the scriptures.

Romans 10:17
So faith comes from what is heard, and what is heard comes by the preaching of Christ.

If you simply believe in something that someone has said then it is not *your* belief; it is someone else's belief. The ownership of our beliefs and faith must be ours, not someone else's. The responsibility for the ownership of our beliefs and faith is ours and no one else's. The problem is that when we think that we know something (in this case, what faith is) we do not bother to check it out. What I am inviting you to do here again is to stop and to check out what faith is for yourself by taking a fresh look at this word and what it really means for you.

The quote from Mark Twain perhaps best summarises, albeit in a very stark way, where many find themselves: believing what they know is not so because they think it is exercising faith. As we take a moment to stand back and think about what many of us find we are (or have been) guilty of, it is incredible to contemplate that we might be caught up in accepting what we actually know *is not* in order to tick the box of faith. What are we saying? That God does not exist but we will have faith in Him anyway? This approach is not only unwise and unhelpful; it is also not what faith is about. So where does this leave us?

Description of Faith

Have you ever found yourself using a word and suddenly discover that you do not actually know what it means or find that it has a different meaning from that which you first thought?

In our context of faith it is important not only to understand and ask what it means but also to understand whether the meaning of the word has changed over time or in translation, in which case we should also ask, what *did* it mean?

The English word 'faith' comes from the Latin *fidem* or *fidēs*, meaning 'trust', derived from the verb *fidere* - 'to trust'. The dictionary defines faith as "an unshakeable trust in something, especially that which cannot be proved."

The important part of this definition is "an unshakeable trust". The English word faith is actually interchangeable with trust. The second part of the definition relates to something that is not proved. It is this part that has caused so many problems. It can be interpreted as 'trusting in something that is not (or cannot be) proved' or alternatively, as it was originally intended, it can be interpreted as 'a trust that although we may not have something tangible in front of us, we know it will come'.

For example, under normal circumstances children trust that their parents will feed them. The food may not be in front of them, they may not be able to see it or smell it, but they know that they will be fed because they have experienced this many times before. Not only that, they know that their friends are also fed because they have talked about it. Of course in abnormal circumstances a child's experience may be different; faith in the parents to provide will be lacking because this is the experience of that particular child.

The Greek word for faith is *pistis* meaning 'trust in others', 'having a confidence and assurance'. Faith is not an intellectual agreement; it is something that comes from our heart. It is reliance. This is the description that the Bible refers to when it defines faith:

Hebrews 11:1

Faith is the assurance of things hoped for, the conviction of things not seen.

In both of these definitions we learn that faith is an unwavering trust in someone or something of which there is no doubt. This is the trust, confidence and assurance of the child brought up in normal circumstances. Based upon the evidence of things learned, seen and experienced, no further tangible proof is needed before it can be applied to a range of situations and circumstances. Faith is not something one has and does 'willy-nilly'. It is a specific, deliberate and calculated act based upon the evidence of things that we see, hear, experience and learn. The source of biblical faith is outlined in Romans:

Romans 10:17

Faith comes from hearing and hearing by the word of Christ.

What Faith Is

To summarise all this in a simple way, faith is *total trust*. In its original Hebrew form the word 'trust' has several meanings, one of which refers to faith-trust. This trust comes from deep within an individual; it comes from the 'heart'. It is a conviction, a knowing or reliant assurance of something that is not necessarily immediately, held because evidence has shown that the trust is justified.

Before we go further we need to understand more about this faith-trust and where it originates from. Unlike the Greek and English language of today, the ancient Hebrew language viewed the world through pictures and the senses, and therefore thought was expressed pictorially through sight, touch, smell, taste and hearing. Concrete words are used to express abstract thoughts, thereby allowing the writer to express the nuances of what they are trying to relate. For example, the following words from the old Hebrew language help us to express the word 'trust' in several different ways in order to draw out subtle differences: *chasah, betach, yachal, aman*. These Hebrew words express the various aspects of trust as:

- A trust that you can lean upon - just as an elderly, frail person can trust a son or daughter by leaning on their arm to walk.
- A trust in which you can find refuge - like a child who can find refuge in their own home away from a bully.
- A trust that you can cling to - in the same way that a child clings to a parent and is nourished and protected by them.
- A trust that you know is assured. This is a faith-trust. It is not hope; it is an assured knowledge that, for example, God will fulfil His promise.
- A trust that is firm. This is the type of firmness that is evident, for example, when you place total trust in someone to be your 'rock', to be secure and reliable.

We all have something or someone that we place our trust, our faith in or upon. Where that trust and faith is placed depends upon our beliefs. It may be, for example, in humanism, a particular person, a religion, an object, in God or in ourselves. The choice is ours to make individually, and the choice is hopefully made based upon evidence concerning the reliability of the thing or person in whom our trust is placed. The more consistent and reliable the source of trust is, the more confident we can be.

With this understanding, the source of faith-knowledge that we have looked at is the Bible. Our faith must be based upon what the Bible says is true. We cannot pick out the bits that we like and leave the bits that we do not like; the Bible is not a 'pick and mix'. Biblical faith is based upon the whole package. Consider the following examples:

John 15: 7

If you abide in me and my words abide in you, you will ask what you desire and it shall be done for you.

This is no empty promise; it is a fact that can be relied upon. We do our part; God does His. It just has to happen.

Matthew 21:22

Whatever you ask in prayer believing, you will receive.

Another promise: ask, believe and receive. It is a sure fact that we must get what we are promised, and so in faith we can wholeheartedly trust God's faithfulness to carry out His words.

If you are looking to find what the heart of faith is, it can be summarised as follows: faith is our response to the Word of God. The evidence for responding to the Word of God and walking in faith is manifested in those who walk in victory and in the authority and resultant power of the Word that can even see the dead rise! I am talking here of the miraculous, awesome power of God that is ours to share if we walk in faith.

Faith is Proactive

I cannot express this point too much or too often and so, dear friend, I do not apologise for repeating in different forms and ways the message that 'faith is proactive' and not, as many so often treat it, simply reactive. Yes, of course there are times when we react to needs by faith, but there is a danger of simply using it this way. James reminds us to...

James 1:22

...be doers of the word, and not hearers only.

In order to understand the impact of what I am trying to say here, let's take a moment to unravel what the word 'proactive' actually means.

Pro in the Greek language means 'before' and so the word *pro*-active means 'before being active'. It is a modern term first used in psychology during the early 1930's and not found in many of the older dictionaries (my 'Collins 1990', for example, does not contain the word). Meanings given today include 'acting in advance of a problem', 'acting with anticipation and initiating change rather than reacting to events' and 'causing something to happen'.

Our faith is firstly placed in God. We know that we can totally trust God; all we need to do is ask and then we can confidently be assured that we have what we have asked for.

Faith is about taking personal responsibility. Once again our understanding of the word 'responsibility' can be heightened as we take a closer look at what it actually means. The second part of the word comes from the word *ible* meaning 'able'. Therefore, responsibility means that we are response-able or 'able to respond'.

Faith is about mobilising our individual free will and decisions. No machine, technology, computer or indeed other human being will ever replace our personal executive decisions and free will. Dear friend, I have come to realise that the responsibility to be proactive and exercise my faith starts and ends with me. Put another way, faith will only be activated with answers following if I do my part and live a life of faith.

Faith is not about what can be gained but about trusting and taking personal responsibility for acting in that trust, using it as a resource no matter what happens. In other words, it is a conviction and commitment that causes the very words that are spoken to reflect total trust in future events or outcomes. Biblical faith in God is very much like this; it rests on the belief and conviction that God cannot break His own word.

In James 2:1-3:12 we find that true faith is evident by impartiality - in other words, by treating everyone in the same way and exercising our faith in love to all no matter who they are. Faith is also evident by our works. By this I mean it is demonstrated in what we do and how we use it. True faith produces changes in our conduct and behaviour. Finally, faith is evident by our words - what we say and how we say it.

The most highly effective positive beliefs and actions are built upon faith. What I am stating again here is that faith is an active process and not, as some think, a passive one where one asks and then proceeds to sit back and wait for the answer. Worse still is that if nothing appears to happen doubt creeps in or the individual begins to find excuses such as 'it wasn't meant to be' or 'it was not God's will'. When was it ever God's will to see people unfit, unhealthy or unhealed?

Faith is about trusting that what you seek and say will happen, and it relies upon the individual doing their part and trusting. In this sense it is the easiest thing that we can do - just trust.

Faith Confusion

Sadly, as a result of poor teaching, attempts to find answers, and explanations based upon personal thought, as well as failure of individuals to personally check for accuracy rather than accept what others may say, the faith language that some use does not reflect the original meaning. In some cases this has led to considerable difficulty and heartache. It is time to call for a reawakening, to place the truth about faith under the microscope and to unravel what lies deep below that which we may currently see on the surface.

As I begin to unwrap aspects of our modern thinking about faith, there may be some about which you ask, "What is the difference?" or suggest, "That is playing with words." The best deflections from the truth are those that are so close that they are almost undetectable; this is why applying tests is so important.

One of the major problems that we have already covered is that of 'blind faith'. This has led to many saying that faith is "the conviction of things not seen" (Hebrews 11:1) and interpreting this to mean that we need no evidence or that we need not do anything except ask God for help and He will provide. This is not only inconsistent with what the Bible says but, as with similar approaches to faith, it can lead to confused outcomes or disappointments, causing more harm than good. Let us remind ourselves that...

Romans 10:17

Faith comes from what is heard, and what is heard comes by the preaching of Christ.

It is from this base and our walk with God that we are convicted by what we have not seen.

Take a moment to consider the following examples.

I read recently a cartoon based upon health. It showed a doctor speaking with his patient who had come in trust and confidence for a check up and help following health issues.

Doctor: Your health issues are affected by your smoking, excessive drinking and poor diet.

Patient: So what are you going to do about it?

A cartoon - but nonetheless a serious message that we each have our part to play.

A friend recently placed a Facebook request saying simply, "I need prayer. I do not want an operation." To my surprise, this simply-stated, short request bothered me, but I could not at first quite grasp what it was that gave me an uneasy feeling. Of course it is right to ask for prayer and there is, let me hasten to add, no problem with prayer and prayer requests. I also did not, in fairness, speak with this friend about their motives and what actions they were taking; therefore I had no real basis upon which to question - and yet my unease persisted.

I pondered long and hard as to why this request had caused me some discomfort and I sought enlightenment. I realised that the request was being made for *others* to pray. Although I recognise that this is not where my friend was coming from, it was being highlighted to me that there is a danger of shifting the problem, like in our doctor and patient example, away from the individual. The individual's faith and responsibility to exercise that faith (by taking appropriate actions) is side-stepped. Yes, faith is about trusting and having confidence, but it also requires us to do our part. I am pleased to say that my friend was asking out of a genuine faith; they were doing their part in coming to God, assured of their healing, and God answered in a most incredible way; my friend was completely healed.

The second example of confusion about faith is often taught, and it goes something like this: "Ask God for whatever your healing need is. Once you have done this, start to proclaim that you have your healing."

So, for example, let's say that you have several warts on the sole of your foot and they are painful to walk upon. This type of faith teaching says, "Even though those warts are there, they can be seen and they hurt you, say, 'No, I asked God to heal them and they have gone.'" This person then says, "I do not have warts on my feet. I asked God to take them and I proclaim them gone; they do not exist."

At best this is simply a misunderstanding of faith and what the Bible teaches; at worse it is a total lie - not only to oneself but also to others. If the warts are still there then they are still there. To claim otherwise is folly; rather we should be saying, "I have asked and God will answer as He promised" or "What is the blockage? What have I not done, or what needs to be done?" or "What can I learn from this, and what other way can I approach the need?"

The faith response should actually be, "I know that God must be true to His word. I have asked for these warts to be healed. They are still there, but I am going to continue to seek what I need, and I will keep knocking at God's door until it has been done."

Matthew 7:7-11

Ask, and it will be given to you; seek, and you will find; knock, and it will be opened to you. For everyone who asks receives, and he who seeks finds, and to him who knocks it will be opened ... If you then, being evil, know how to give good gifts to your children, how much more will your Father who is in heaven give good things to those who ask Him!

If faith is based upon evidence (just as the evidence of Jesus' miracles enables us to trust God and what He says) then it makes no sense to continue to trust that a healing has taken place when the sickness is still evident. The response should surely be one of integrity: "The healing has not taken place yet, but God is true to His word." We should also be saying, "What can I do differently to achieve my request and aim? What more does God want?"

Although it is a basic requirement, it is not enough to simply say, "Have faith!" We also need to know what faith is, what it means to have faith, how we can exercise faith and how we can improve our faith.

Jesus and Faith

In exploring aspects of faith we have, until now, mostly viewed faith from our earthly perspective and through our earthly eyes and experience. It is from this viewpoint that those of good intention have launched out mistakenly thinking that this is a position of sufficiency. The result has been that all too often the very things that have been prayed for and believed for have not come to fruition and we have wondered why. In the healing ministry many dear souls have been upset and hurt as they have seen those close to them failing to receive the promises of God - their healing.

Faith is not about making verbal statements or claims based on mental beliefs. It is not like using a formula or heeding to a set of words. Faith is about a relationship with God. It is about walking in obedience and taking hold of God's words and promises. It is about walking in the authority that God bestows upon us and in the name of the Lord Jesus Christ.

What I am talking about is a faith level that is supernatural - a level at which one enters the very depths of heaven itself. It requires a walk so close to God that it changes the person that we are. It is a walk that mimics the very life of Jesus so that, as we read in Hebrews 12:2, we are "looking to Jesus, the pioneer and perfecter of our faith". It is in and through Jesus that we learn how to activate our faith, and it is through Jesus that our faith is perfected

When we see faith at work through Jesus and his disciples, we see them in assured authority. They know who they are and they know that God is all-powerful, all-loving and compassionate. It is an assurance that God will release the Holy Spirit in power; so when they seek a healing or a miracle, the language that they use is direct, said with conviction and with the authority of God Himself.

The message of the gospel and healing, miracles, signs and wonders are closely linked. When healings take place faith is exercised as a command, not a long-winded prayer. It is through supernatural faith that the impossible becomes possible, for as Jesus said:

Mark 9:23

All things are possible to him who believes.

Supernatural faith comes as we please God through our faith, humility and obedience. The prophet Enoch walked so closely with God and pleased Him that "he was not, for God took him" (Genesis 5: 24).

Smith Wigglesworth once said:

Great faith is the product of great fights. Great testimonies are the outcome of great tests. Great triumphs come only out of great trials. Every stumbling block must become a stepping stone, and every opposition must become an opportunity.

Great faith - supernatural faith - is not born from giving up at every difficulty. It is rooted in knowing God and building a total trust in Him.

Examples of Faith

Hebrews 1-11 both explains faith and provides examples of the faith of the early patriarchs (whom I would encourage you to research more intently.) For our purposes here, and in order to gain an understanding of what faith is, let's take a brief journey into a couple of examples that are laid out for us in the major source book that we have available: the Bible.

Noah (Genesis 6:13-22)

We read prior to this text that God had despaired in trying to communicate with people, who instead were moving by their own free choice away from Him. God spoke to Noah telling him of an impending flood and giving details of how and where to build an ark plus what should be contained within.

Noah could have ignored God. There was no proof of an impending flood, but in faith Noah knew that God was true to His word. He trusted God's word and did as he was instructed.

Lame Man Healed (Acts 14:8-10)

Here we read of a man who had been crippled from birth. He came to hear Paul preaching. The man had faith that he would be healed, and on being called upon to stand, did not hesitate but got up and walked.

In these examples and in many, many more, we see that...

- Faith originates in someone having learned that God is who He says He is.
- Someone trusts God to do as He says He will.
- Someone acts upon the trust and what God says.

It is all very well to have faith, but it is useless without actually applying it and using it. It's a bit like having a torch in the pitch black and not turning it on to see what you are doing and where you are going. Faith also grows and develops through use or, as Smith Wigglesworth put it, "Great faith is the result of great fights."

Faith is a Resource

Faith is a necessary part of our daily living, something that we all carry with us as a trusty resource and upon which we can call at any time - using it to protect, defend or deflect in times of need, whatever that need may be.

When, under what circumstances, how often, how and why we call upon the resource of faith varies from one person to another. How effective, how large and how strong our faith is depends upon what or in whom we have built our faith as well as how well we have developed, honed and looked after that faith.

Let's take a closer look at some of the typical times when the resource of faith is called upon:

- In times of danger
- In times of sickness
- In times of despair and hopelessness
- In times when the world seems to be falling around us

Once again, here we can see that faith is not meant to be a passive part of our lives. In biblical terms it is referred to as a shield and is called 'the shield of faith' in Ephesians. There we are instructed to..

Ephesians 6:16
Take the shield of faith, with which you can quench all the flaming darts of the evil one.

The shield is actively used. It is put in place *before* the 'flaming darts' are hurled, not afterward. It can also be moved to deflect from whatever direction we need to place it. It is meant to be used!

The quality, strength, reliability and effectiveness of our faith source are like the properties of our shield. We can choose its size and what it is made out of. How long would a riot policeman last if he chose a sixty centimetre shield made of glass? It would be folly to do so. Equally, the source of our faith must be carefully selected; in Mark 11:22 we are told, "Have faith in God."

Faith Metaphor

Coming from a sports background it is quite natural for me to consider issues in relation to sport and sport situations. Sport has often been used as an illustration of life situations such as working with others, accepting defeat, abiding by the rules, achieving our goals and so on.

As an example, I see parallels between the game of golf and life, perhaps more than with many other sports; playing golf can be like using and applying faith.

The golf coach is someone who is there to teach, to correct, to help, to guide, to support and to show the way. It is necessary for the golf player to have trust in, and spend time with, their coach as well as to consistently hone the skills taught and required to become a good player.

It is also necessary for players to practice and play regularly in order to maintain their confidence and finer skills, knowing what type of shot and which golf club is most useful for different situations and circumstances. All this however is not enough - as any golfer will tell you. What you think, believe and do are crucial elements of the game. Things can go wrong, disappointments can arise, but a good player will leave that at the last hole and start over again on the next.

The golfer knows what they want to achieve. They consider carefully each shot and they try to avoid the hazards. Hazards have a habit, however, of getting in the way, especially when poor shots or poor decisions are made. It is important that the player recognises their mistake, takes responsibility for their own actions and views these in a positive light. The situation is obviously more difficult, but the mindset and actions are the same.

Of course, some hazards are more challenging, such as water hazards. The player needs to take a penalty shot - a step (or sometimes many steps) backward. This is not a time to give up. It is a time to re-consider the previous shot, the club used, the angle of play etc. and move forward - to learn from the mistake rather than seeing it as a failure and to get back on track.

The Rules of Faith and Harnessing its Power

Whether looking at faith from a biblical or non-biblical viewpoint the principles are the same. The only difference is in whom or in what you place your faith. There are a number of faith rules that need to be followed.

If you are a Christian, the first rule is to believe that God is who He says He is. Take a look at this verse:

Mark 11:22-26

And Jesus answered them, "Have faith in God. Truly, I say to you, whoever says to this mountain, 'Be taken up and cast into the sea', and does not doubt in his heart, but believes that what he says will come to pass, it will be done for him. Therefore, I tell you, whatever you ask in prayer, believer that you have received it, and it will be yours. And whenever you stand praying, forgive, if you have anything against any one; so that your Father also who is in heaven may forgive you your trespasses."

In verse 22 we see the source of faith: faith in God
In verse 23 we discover three incredible truths:

- The source of faith is assured; it is true. There is no doubt regarding its reliability.
- Faith is activated by and through what we say.

- Faith and doubt are extremely poor bedfellows. You cannot have faith on the one hand and doubt on the other. Doubt destroys faith.

These verses mean that we can be totally confident that we will receive that which we ask for in faith. As a confirmation, the next verse, 24, states that the individual who asks, then exercises their faith and believes, will get what they requested. When we exercise faith we establish a two-way contract that is between God and us.

Verses 25 and 26 explain the basis upon which we should make our requests: forgiveness.

Faith and Forgiveness

A sure way to hinder the flow of God's blessings is to lack love and forgiveness. What happened inside you when the word 'forgive' rang out? Did you immediately feel a resistance? Did you think, "You do not understand my situation"?

An unforgiving heart is a heart of darkness. Being hardhearted, critical and unforgiving will, as sure as 'eggs are eggs', create a blockage in the flow of faith and God's ability to work. God cannot walk in darkness, and He cannot be unequally bound with us if we are unforgiving.

Unforgiveness not only separates us from God; it also, if left unattended, grows and spreads.

Hebrews 12:15

See to it that no one fail to obtain the grace of God; that no 'root of bitterness' spring up and cause trouble, and by it many become defiled.

If there is unforgiveness, take immediate action and deal with it; otherwise no amount of tears will move God.

Having established the source of biblical faith, the basic rules are to *speak* it, *believe* it and *do* it.

Let me be honest with you. I have over many years grappled to align what I have read about faith with what I have seen in both others' and my own life. The Bible makes some incredible statements saying that if I apply my faith I can ask God for whatever I want or need and He will provide it.

The statements are clear and yet, in truth, I have not always seen the reality.

I have been left with the thought that either the words recorded in the Bible are untrue or I have not used the right key to open the treasure box. I am, if I am being true and honest to myself, personally unable to find evidence in my life experiences to deny God because amidst the unpleasant things (my failed plea for my father's life and those dark moments) there have been times of blessing and protection. It is not God that is at fault but me. As the American comedian Fred Allen (1894 – 1956) is attributed as once saying, I have acted as if I can...

Spend the first six days of the week sowing wild oats,
Then go to church on Sunday and pray for a crop failure

I have used faith inappropriately, thinking that I could go around in my own way and that it was something to call upon only in times of need. As I became aware of how successful people live their lives I noticed that it was exactly as the Bible was outlining; many of these people did not have a God-faith but they were applying the same principles. It dawned on me that I too should follow these principles.

I can remember sitting with my wife talking about what we wanted in a house. We decided to write down all of the things that we wanted and then began to search for a property. We had no doubt about getting a new home. We talked about what we wanted. We pictured it in our minds. We believed we would get what we wanted and we searched high and low for it - even coming close to taking something that was a compromise rather than pressing on to what we really wanted. We ended up with something that actually was *more* than we had first sought and asked for.

What do highly successful people do? We can learn much from following these very simple rules:

- They find something to place their purpose in. (Faith in God is the way of a Christian life.)
- They take responsibility for their own actions.
- They say (confess) what they want. They have clearly outlined goals.

- They believe and accept that what they have asked for they will get.
- They act upon what they have asked for.
- They tell others about what they have asked for.
- They maintain integrity.

On a recent holiday visit to the lovely Provence fishing town of Cassis, whilst walking through the busy streets, I saw someone wearing a T-shirt on the back of which it said:

If you do not live for something
You die for nothing

Apart from possibly being a corruption of Rambo's punch-line "Live for nothing or die for something", I am not sure where this quote originates. However, the sentiment rings true. We all have abilities and the potential to overcome difficulties, achieving our inner desires or goals, rather than living defeated through lack of faith. It is far better to exercise faith than to live in helplessness.

Procrastination

One of the biggest diseases in human behaviour with regard to achievement and attaining one's potential is that of procrastination - the counterproductive 'putting off' of actions or tasks.

There are various reasons that people procrastinate, including the following:

- Perfectionism – They cannot do something well, so they do not do it at all.
- Lack of belief – They do not believe they can do it.
- Fear – They are afraid of the unknown or of failure.
- Lack of effort – They 'cannot be bothered' and so are not willing to try.
- Lack of faith / trust – They do not believe that it will happen and succeed.
- Conflict – They have conflicting priorities and unclear aims.

Whatever the reason for procrastination, the interesting thing is that if a person tries whatever it is that they are seeking for one minute it is likely that they will continue a little longer and even keep going. The message is to try it and keep going, but I know from my own experience (and certainly from that of others) that struggles may still continue.

Faith Pleases God

The fact is, as we have discovered already, faith pleases God (Hebrews 11:6). There are so many examples in the Bible of Jesus responding emphatically where faith is shown (Mark 5:34, Mark 10:52, Luke 17:19) and we are told that the exercise of faith will have an assured outcome (Mark 11:23).

The bottom line is that the exercise of faith must produce a result - God has to be true to His Word - so if we do not see a result then we must ask why. This question will require us to examine our motives, beliefs and actions. The first point is... are we asking? This may seem strange but there are many times when we simply do not ask - maybe out of fear, maybe out of feelings of unworthiness or simply because we do not know that we can ask. The other side to this is that of asking out of an impure heart, desire and covetousness.

James 4:2,3
You do not have because you do not ask. You ask and do not receive, because you ask wrongly, to spend it on your passions.

The question in these instances is not 'why?' but 'what is your heart when you come to God?'

I was recently listening to a Youtube sermon by a well-respected, well-known, faithful international minister, David Wilkerson (1931-2011). He was talking about how God knows about our pains, afflictions and struggles, heavy hearts concerning the illness of a loved one or their financial problems, and so many other afflictions. This moving and God-fearing message left me asking, "Is it enough to say that God knows? God has spoken so clearly about the positive exercise of faith, and here I am brought before a man who has served God faithfully, who knows pain not only in himself but through a sick wife, son and daughter. Not only does he know suffering, he is a man who recognises the anguish of our thoughts as we question God asking, "Why?" understanding the doubts that cross our minds; yet he continues to trust in God's care."

At this point I wish that I could give you an answer so that suffering, pain and sickness would be immediately taken away. The fact is that God never promised us an easy ride. Just as Jesus himself suffered, so we will also face sufferings because we are in a battle; the battle is for our souls, and Satan is out to get us in any way that he can. We are warned by Peter to stick to the hope that we have in Christ:

1 Peter 5:8,9

Be sober, be watchful. Your adversary the devil prowls around like a roaring lion, seeking someone to devour. Resist him, firm in your faith, knowing that the same experience of suffering is required of your brotherhood throughout the world.

It is not my desire to question another person's beliefs, but for me, deep down in my heart and as I read the scriptures, I cannot totally grasp the fact that the Bible clearly makes such statements as:

- Ask and you will receive.
- Whatever you ask in my Name I will do it.
- Have faith in God, for assuredly you will.

And yet far too often we do not see the reality of these promises.

These are positive, uncompromising statements. If we ask we will receive. In terms of illness and sickness, Jesus turned no one away; all were healed. Are we to accept that none of this applies to the Christian because they have to suffer and not have the promises of God?

Yes, difficulties do exist and, yes, we will face them; but is sickness to be acceptable in the body of Christ? I am sorry; I just do not see this in the Bible. I do not have all of the answers, but I have to be faithful to what I read.

As we look at the life of Jesus it is clear that he often confronted head-on the work of Satan that was, and still is today, manifested through infirmity, sickness, disease, fear and demon possession. On every face-off between Jesus and Satan, Jesus was the victor. Why? Because:

1 John 3:8

The reason the Son of God appeared was to destroy the works of the devil.

By crushing the control that Satan placed on people through sicknesses and possession he weakened their resolve, but Jesus released captives and brought freedom and life.

The whole point about faith is to remain totally committed to God and to trust Him no matter what happens. This is truly a time not to turn away from Christ; we need to be on our guard against bitterness and fear for these will harden our hearts against God. If you ever wanted to understand why faith is so pleasing to God and why He will always reward it then 'faithfulness through adversary' is your clue.

Double-Mindedness

During the course of this chapter we have explored various things that may lead to blockages in our 'faith' channel to God. Here we come across a major reason for blockage - that of double-mindedness.

In the letter of James we find quite a lot written about faith. Here James makes it clear that faith is not simply about believing. It is not a passive thing but rather it is alive and vibrant, being manifested through our actions and works. We also discover that James has a few words to say about the stability of our faith-thoughts and our minds, so let's take a few moments to see what the Bible has to say about being double-minded:

James 1: 6-8

Ask in faith, with no doubting, for he who doubts is like a wave of the sea that is driven and tossed by the wind. For that person must not suppose that a double-minded man, unstable in all his ways, will receive anything from the Lord.

In this scripture we see that if our faith is not producing results we need to take a long, hard and honest look at what we say and think and also how we act. Does doubt manifest itself in any of these areas?

If doubt is a lingering thought, James offers these words:

James 1:22-25
Be doers of the Word, and not hearers only, deceiving yourselves. For if anyone is a hearer of the word and not a doer, he is like a man who observes his natural face in a mirror, for he observes himself and goes away and at once forgets what he was like. But he who looks into the perfect law, the law of liberty, and perseveres, being no hearer that forgets but a doer that acts, he shall be blessed in his doing.

We are required to apply our faith, to use it, practice it, trust it, for our faith is in God. The more we do this, the more it will come naturally to us. As we see the results of our faith, it encourages us in times of difficulty. Our part is to have faith in God. God's part is to act upon our faith as He knows best. This may not be what we want to hear, but it is what we are required to do and be.

Using Faith Language

We have already established that words contain power; they contain energy and a message that creates a reactive response. This is no less true when the language that we apply to faith is used.

How many times do you set out on a journey without knowing where you are going? Faith is not about drifting without a purpose. It is not about 'leaving it to God' to decide your path. It is important to know what you want and to be very specific about what it is that you want.

Using the auditory, visual and kinaesthetic senses we can increase the effectiveness of our language:

Auditory
Verbalise / say what you want / what you believe.
Clearly express your want, need or belief.
Describe in detail what you want.

State your purpose.

Speak to your mind / speak to God.

Visual

Visualise what you want – see it.

Catch a glimpse of what it is like to have what you want.

Make the picture of what you want clear and bright.

Kinaesthetic

Feel / touch it.

Use your faith as a firm foundation.

Hold on tight to your request – do not let it go.

Grab your opportunities with both hands.

Walking in Faith

Faith is a daily walk and exercise which begins each morning with a simple offering of ourselves to God and a trust in His faithfulness toward us as we are faithful toward Him.

I talked earlier about one of my favourite Bible verses, Mark 11:22-26. In verse 23 we read, "and does not doubt in his heart." This has often been a phrase that has exercised my thoughts. As I sat again and grappled with this it occurred to me that love and faith are so tightly knit together. Just as love flows from our heart so faith also flows. As our love for God grows our trust and faith increase, and as our faith increases our prayers become bolder and more meaningful. There ceases to be room for doubt; our hearts are filled with love and faith, which ooze from our very presence.

Romans 8:28

We know that in everything God works for good with those who love Him, who are called according to His purpose.

We can be totally assured that God will fulfil His promises to us - that is, all of the promises that He makes in the Bible. As I mentioned earlier in this chapter, Jesus made an incredible, almost mind-blowing statement when he said that greater works will be done by those of us who believe in him than the works that he performed. Come with me and take a closer look at this statement.

John 14:12-14

Truly, truly, I say to you, he who believes in me will also do the works that I do; and greater works than these will he do, because I go to the Father. Whatever you ask in my name, I will do it, that the Father may be glorified in the Son, if you ask anything in my name, I will do it.

The statement by Jesus not only starts with 'truly' but Jesus repeats it: "Truly, truly." It's like us saying today, "Honestly, I can assure you there is no doubt." If we believe, we are told that we will not only do the works that Jesus did - all those healings and miracles - but even greater things! What a staggering promise and awesome responsibility we have to ask in the name of Jesus!

Smith Wigglesworth once said that we should stir ourselves to a point where we realise that we are responsible for the needs that exist around us. God has promised to meet and supply not only our needs but also those of others around us. Failure to meet these needs is, as Wigglesworth went on to say, a tragedy. We have the life and the promise of the powerful name of Jesus in us, and therefore we have what it takes to see miracles happen.

I do not know about you, but I have come to realise that my thinking has been wrong. I have, as I had thought was only right to do, asked and pleaded for an anointing and a move of the Holy Spirit upon me in order to kick-start me with power. Please hear me out - it is not wrong to do this. But if we spend our time waiting and doing nothing, failing to use and exercise our faith, we may 'miss the boat' completely. Part of our daily walk with God is to flex our faith muscles in the name of Jesus. It is about being bold, acting upon God's word and allowing Him to release His power as He wills. It is when we do this that we are truly walking in faith. It is not up to you or me to concern ourselves about outcomes but rather to listen to God, obey His word and act upon these.

Faith is an essential quality requiring perseverance - constantly seeking God, not letting go of His promises and being assured of blessing. When faith is tested it develops perseverance (James 1:2,3). Let us not be tardy in our use of faith or concerned if things get tough. If God makes a promise or He says that something will happen, it will happen.

The measure of what we receive in our faith walk is in proportion to our faith. No matter who we are, we will always get what we believe.

4. The Language of Prayer

When asked how much time he spent in prayer, George Muller's reply was, 'Hours every day. But I live in the spirit of prayer. I pray as I walk and when I lie down and when I arise. And the answers are always coming.'

- Origin unknown -

Introduction

During the course of this book I have tackled a series of key issues that relate to a release of the power of miracles in our lives and bring health and healing to our spiritual and physical life. Given the topics covered and the purposes behind this publication, I cannot leave out the key role that prayer and daily communion with God have in the life of each and every Christian believer.

The importance of prayer is illustrated by the fact that the words 'prayer', 'pray', 'prayed', and 'praying' appear throughout the Bible from the opening book Genesis through to Revelation over 500 times. Indeed, Paul enthusiastically states:

Romans 12:12

Rejoice in your hope, be patient in tribulation, be constant [some versions say 'faithful'] in prayer.

We are urged to be constant or faithful in prayer; but do we know what prayer actually is and why it is so important? Is prayer a Christian's crisis tool for times of need, or is there more to it? Above all, do we know how to pray and receive answers?

Have you ever stopped and asked yourself, "What exactly is prayer?" If I am honest, I thought that this was a simple question to answer, and indeed at its simplest level it is quite straightforward. That was until I read something that Smith Wigglesworth had said:

I pray into the very heart of God.

As Smith prayed, observers said that God's presence would fall. Smith could walk by people in the street, and they would come under the conviction of the Holy Spirit. This got me thinking about that phrase and how it was that Smith was not just praying but praying into the *very heart of God*. What did this mean and how did Smith go about doing it?

Smith Wigglesworth understood that he could only do reach into God's heart by loving God, filling his head and heart with the word of God and daily walking by faith with God. His prayers were audacious and he prayed in openness to, and through the guidance and help of, the Holy Spirit.

Romans 8:25-28

But if we hope for what we do not see, with perseverance we wait eagerly for it. And in the same way the Spirit also helps our weakness for we do not know how to pray as we should, but the Spirit himself intercedes for us with groaning too deep for words; and He who searches the hearts knows what the mind of the Spirit is, because He intercedes for the saints according to the will of God.

The Holy Spirit intercedes for us in ways that are beyond any words that we can use. The Holy Spirit takes the essential parts of our prayers - those that match the will of God - and turns these prayers into powerhouses. Prayers that are prayed without the Holy Spirit will never be enough, and so we are told to pray in the Spirit every time we pray:

Ephesians 6:18

Pray at all times in the Spirit, with all pray and supplication.

Smith was asked one day what his secret was concerning walking in God's power - something that was clearly demonstrated in his life. His insightful and telling response was, "A broken and contrite heart." Smith loved his wife, who had died leaving him broken-hearted and alone. He carried that pain whilst also unshakeably trusting God. He never once blamed God or drifted from his love of God.

Psalm 51:17

The sacrifices of God are a broken spirit: a broken and contrite heart, O God, you will not despise.

Wow! I do not know how that leaves you. To be honest it really scares me, and I hope that I do not face anything like that which Smith went through. Still, there is a part of me that says I am prepared to have a broken spirit - a broken and contrite heart that does not hinder God's flow through my life.

Despite his uncompromising attitudes and, in the view of some bystanders, his forceful personality, Smith was a man of compassion. So deep was his love for God and for those around him that it has been described, as we have already seen, that Smith was able to pray to the very heart of God because he devoted himself in prayer. What Smith understood was that prayer matters and prayer changes things. He understood that he needed to know what God wanted him to do and not to rely upon his own instincts and desires.

My path has been perhaps a little easier than Smith's, but I am ashamed to admit that over the years I have hurt God, my family and my friends because of my disobedience and sinfulness. I am claiming nothing at all other than to share that I, sinner as I am, have come to a point where I can no longer say 'no' to allowing God to bring His fire into my heart and spirit, to break me and to mould me as I humble myself before Him.

In being open to God's fire, what has become prophetically clear to me is that a time is coming when a mighty outpouring of the Holy Spirit, greater than the pockets of outpourings that have taken place worldwide so far, is imminent. This outpouring needs the prayer of those who pray mountain-moving prayers. I am open to be used by God as He desires and to do as He says. My prayer is that God will use this book to stir in your heart His words and a supernatural thirst and hunger to be part of His revival and to do whatever He says to you. Prayer that reaches the heart of God through love, faith and the Holy Spirit will unlock untold power.

Amongst those numbered as the greatest men of prayer we find the American Methodist Episcopal church minister Edward McKendree Bounds (1835 – 1913), usually simply known as E. M. Bounds, who wrote what many consider to be the greatest book on prayer ever written: 'Power Through Prayer'. In this book he wrote:

> *What the Church needs today is not more machinery or better, not new organizations or more and novel methods, but men whom the Holy Ghost can use -- men of prayer, men mighty in prayer. The Holy Ghost does not flow through methods, but through men. He does not come on machinery, but on men. He does not anoint plans, but men -- men of prayer.*

One of the characteristics behind all mighty moves of God and behind all revivals is a solid base of prayer. My dear friend, this is an opportunity to be part of God's will, to break open untold treasures from the heart of God and to allow Him to move in mighty ways through our love, faith and prayers. It is important that we learn what prayer really is and, importantly, how to pray in power.

So What is Prayer?

If a survey of this question would be taken and people asked to reply, most of the answers would probably be along the lines that prayer is our communication with God by means of the spoken or sung word or in meditation through internal dialogue. The outwardly spoken or sung form of prayer can either be from the individual to God or it can be communal, shared with others who are listening, or they may even join the prayer such as repeating the Lord's Prayer on mass.

Some people might give a fuller response and add that prayer takes many forms such as the repetition of pre-prepared or prescribed rote prayers, petition, supplication, entreaty, confession, adoration and thanksgiving.

For many people prayer is something that is done when a need arises and there is no other place to go. This is a bit like going to a heavenly shop to take what is on the shelf that meets our need. There is no relationship involvement; it is simply a means to an end.

That all sounds accurate, covering just about every aspect of prayer - or does it? Is there more that we need to know about prayer? Have we really understood what prayer is and how to pray? Is all this really good enough?

Take a closer look at what the Bible says about prayer. Prayer is not something we just do at certain times of the day or when we go to church. It is not a soliloquy; it is a dialogue, a conversation. It is just like having a close friend - we chat together, we share thoughts, we ask questions. We also speak with our friend in times of need and they listen, they give support, they comfort us with their words and they give answers to help us.

Prayer is our means of direct communication with a loving, awesome, merciful God with whom we wish to deepen our relationship. Put another way, prayer *is* a relationship with God - it is our lifeline, lifeblood and link with God maintained by being open and honest, asking forgiveness for the hurts we have caused, sharing our thoughts, seeking help, and pleading for mercy and healing for ourselves as well as others. Prayer is also a place of rest, reflection, listening and growing in love; a place to seek information, direction and advice. Prayer is a dynamic, the powerhouse where miracles are released. Walking with God and making prayer an indispensable part of one's life moves the heart of God to respond as we ask. Yes, prayer has an enormous effect. Why do I say this? Take a look at what James had to say:

James 5:16-18

The prayer of a righteous man has great power in its effects. Elijah was a man of like nature with ourselves and he prayed fervently that it might not rain, and for three years and six months it did not rain on the earth. Then he prayed again and the heaven gave rain, and the earth brought forth its fruit.

If our prayers do not get results we are often too quick to blame God rather than to take a look at ourselves.

Listen to God

Do we leave time and opportunity for God to speak and to answer? So often we make our requests known to God, we speak with Him, but we do not let Him speak to us; prayer ends up being at best a monologue and at worse a repetitive monotone. We then complain that God has not answered. I have certainly been guilty of misusing and misunderstanding prayer, mainly out of ignorance, being caught up in tradition and poor teaching. How else can we know what God is saying if we do not determine to listen to what He has to say both through meditation in scripture and through allowing Him time to speak to our spirit through the Holy Spirit in us? We need to attune ourselves to God speaking, for if we do not listen to God we may well end up listening elsewhere and open ourselves to being deceived. Take a moment to consider what would have happened if Noah had not listened to God. He would have drowned! How did Noah know God was talking to him?

Genesis 6:9

Noah walked with God.

Prayer is also a form of communication with God that is *supported*. In Hebrews 7:25 we see that Jesus intercedes for us, and in Romans 8:26 the Holy Spirit also intercedes for us. What does this mean? The word 'intercede' means 'to intervene, mediate or reconcile differences by speaking on behalf of someone'. When we pray, we do not do so alone, for our prayers are taken by the Holy Spirit who intercedes or speaks on our behalf; that is why we are told in Ephesians 6:18 to pray at all times in the Spirit. This is worth saying again: our prayers should be *prayed in the Spirit at all times*. George Muller, in our opening quotation, explained this by saying that he lived in the Spirit of prayer.

Learning to Pray

There are many great people of God that have reportedly stated that they spend, for example, two or three hours in prayer every day. This is great and wonderful, but is this pattern one that we should emulate? I am not convinced that we have here the whole picture, and I am also not convinced that those who haven spoke of such practice followed a prayer life quite as prescribed and defined as this.

There is a danger that we either fall into condemnation, feeling unworthy, or that we pray according to a pattern and convince ourselves that we have fulfilled what is required of us in our prayer life. Both of these are wrong. Let's take a closer look at what the Bible has to say.

There is no record that Jesus simply spent daily prescribed times in prayer. His *life* was prayer. He spent whatever time was necessary and it was continuous. Certainly, there are times when Jesus spent long periods in concentrated or focussed prayer, and the Bible informs us that...

Luke 5:16
He ... would often slip away to the wilderness and pray.

The long periods that Jesus spent in prayer were related to specific events such as the choosing of the disciples:

Luke 6:12
And it was at this time that He went off to the mountain to pray, and He spent the whole night in prayer to God.

Jesus also told us that he only did what His father's will was (for example, John 4:34, John 6:38, Matthew 26:39). To know what the Father's will was, Jesus must have remained in constant communication. Certainly, we read about this kind of prayer in the word of God:

Ephesians 6:18
Pray at all times in the Spirit, with all prayer and supplication.

Here it is disclosed that there are different types of prayer including prayer for help. And again we read:

1 Thessalonians 5:17
Pray constantly.

What are we learning here? Jesus prayed and his life was prayer. He went and talked with His father. He sought advice and help from His father. He sought His father's wishes. He simply went and spent time in

His father's presence, chatting and listening. Notice that this was a two-way conversation, that they spent alone and together.

Prayer was also something that Jesus did as a matter of course in His daily life and with others. He prayed at the start of His ministry:

Luke 3:21,22
And while He was praying, heaven was opened and the Holy Spirit descended on Him in a bodily form like a dove.

We read that Jesus prayed for His disciples, He prayed for the sick, He prayed for children, He prayed for us. If Jesus had need to pray then how much more do we?

The prayer life of Jesus was essentially a continuous communication interspersed with specific requests. It was the kind of good relationship that we might have with our friends, children with their parents, married couples with one another, and so on. In these special relationships there are times when we have short conversations - sharing, asking advice, helping, posing questions and seeking answers, making comments in passing. These are, however, interspersed with lengthy, in-depth discussions when we need to share specific needs, and lengths of time spent with one another to develop a bond. Sometimes we need to say 'sorry' and know that we are loved.

We gain precious insight from the letter to the Hebrews:

Hebrews 5:7
In the days of his flesh, Jesus offered up prayers and supplications, with loud cries and tears, to him who was able to save him from death, and he was heard for his godly fear.

The disciples were so aware of the example that Jesus demonstrated in His prayer life and the powerful effects of His prayer that they asked:

Luke 11:1
Lord, teach us to pray.

Jesus outlined how the disciples should pray:

Luke 11:2-4 (RSV)

Father, hallowed be Thy name, Thy kingdom come. Give us each day our daily bread. And forgive us our sins, for we ourselves also forgive everyone who is indebted to us. And lead us not into temptation.

This prayer recognises who God is, His Holiness and fact that we can address Him as Father in the same way that Jesus did. In other words, we are counted as children of God. Just as with a good father-child relationship, this prayer also deals with our general needs, our need to forgive and seek forgiveness and our need for protection against temptation and the evil one.

In Matthew, before the 'Lord's Prayer', we learn some important lessons about praying:

Matthew 6:5-8

And when you pray, you must not be like the hypocrites; for they love to stand and pray in the synagogues and at the street corners, that they may be seen by men. Truly, I say to you, they have received their reward. But when you pray, go into your room and shut the door and pray to your Father who is in secret; and your Father who sees in secret will reward you. And in praying do not heap up empty phrases as the Gentiles do; for they think that they will be heard for their many words. Do not be like them, for your Father knows what you need before you ask him!

Prayer is not about showmanship - seeking adoration and respect from onlookers as to how devout we are. Jesus called this type of praying hypocritical and said that the onlookers, not God, will reward this type of prayer. So armed with this background information, how do we pray prayers that touch the very heart of God?

Prayers that Move God

Let's take a look at Ezra's example:

Ezra 10:1

While Ezra prayed and made confession, weeping and casting himself down before the house of God, a very great assembly of men, women and children, gathered to him out of Israel; for the people wept bitterly.

The very first thing that Ezra did was to confess his sins. He confessed before the very throne of God that he personally, along with his fellow Israelites, had sinned. More than just sin, it was sin directly against God, since he had not adhered to His commandments. So deep was this conviction of sin that Ezra felt total shame and humility before God. He said:

Ezra 9:6

O my God, I am ashamed and blush to lift my face to thee, my God.

As we read this story we are also struck by the faithfulness that God had shown His people. Ezra was clearly moved by the love that God had given - even when He had been let down God had offered a hand of love.

So moved was Ezra that he wept before God. Dear friend, how often have we wept tears like this before God? These are tears of a realisation that our sins and the sins of those around us are truly sins against God himself. If the evil we see around us and the deceptions and failings in our very churches do not cause us to weep, our shame before God is not realised.

Ezra then made a promise to God, taking other leaders with him, to turn from their failings, to repent and to reconcile with God (Ezra 10:3-5). This was followed by a time of fasting. So upset was Ezra that he could not eat (Ezra 10:6).

Faith is also an important part of prayer. James tells us:

James 1:6-8

But let him ask in faith, with no doubting, for he who doubts is like a wave of the sea that is driven and tossed by the wind. For that person must not suppose that a double-minded man, unstable in all his ways, will receive anything from the Lord.

When we pray, our prayers should be specific and our requests made with complete confidence that God will answer. 'Wishy-washy' prayers are not prayers of faith and, as James points out, they will not provide answers. How many times do we pray apologetic, weak prayers? How many times do we pray for the sick asking for everything but their total healing? In Matthew 17:20 we read about an occasion when the disciples had prayed for a young boy to be cured but nothing had happened. On asking Jesus why, the reply was short, to the point and totally unexpected: "Because of your little faith." Jesus then went on to say something even more astounding. "If you have faith as a grain of mustard seed, you will say to this mountain, 'move from here to there', and it will move; and nothing will be impossible to you." The smallest amount of faith exercised in prayer will produce incredible results.

What we learn from this story and our journey so far are some key steps in praying prayers that reach the very depths of heaven itself:

- Confession
- Repentance
- Forgiveness
- Tears
- Faith
- Holy Spirit

We will never move the heart of God in our prayers like Wigglesworth, Muller and so many others unless our prayer life and prayers match these biblical examples.

The Psalmist David, speaking of separation from God, demonstrated his anguish. A prayerless or weak prayer life is one of separated times from God. We should be able to say, feel and experience the same anguish that David felt when he said:

Psalm 42:1-3

As a hart longs for the flowing steams, so longs my soul for thee, O God. My soul thirst for God, for the living God. When shall I come and behold the face of God? My tears have been my food day and night.

Communal Prayer

Does all of this suggest that we should not be praying in the church as a group? This is a good question and we need to carefully check what the Bible has to say. Certainly we must be aware of our motives, and the eloquence, length or abundance of a person's communal prayer should not attract us. It is more about the relationship that each person has with God and the earnestness, devotion and unity of these prayers.

When Peter was retained in prison the church came together in earnest prayer.

Acts 12:5
So Peter was kept in prison; but earnest prayer for him was made to God by the church.

Again we read that when Peter and John were set free the church met together.

Acts 4:31
And when they had prayed, the place in which they were gathered together was shaken; and they were all filled with the Holy Spirit.

When the disciples met together with Mary, the brothers of Jesus and other women they devoted themselves to prayer.

Acts 1:14
All these with one accord devoted themselves to prayer.

The power of the unity of communal prayer is suggested in Jesus' words:

Matthew 18:20
...for where two or three are gathered in my name, there am I in the midst of them.

The basis of prayer is the same whether as an individual or as a group. Group prayer is highly effective in its earnestness, unity, devotion and accord. It is about having one focus and giving honour to God. It is not about empty words and phrases. It is not about eloquence and it is not about focus or admiration for any one individual's ability or prayer.

Developing Prayer Skills

My experience in the field of sport has shown that the only way to become good at a sport and develop skills is to practice. The sportsperson has to be devoted to the sport, practicing daily for many hours and seeking help from the coach.

Prayer is no different; it requires practice:

- Romans 12:12 – "...devoted to prayer..."
- Ephesians 6:8 – "...pray at all times in the Spirit."
- Colossians 4:2 – "Devote yourself to prayer, keeping alert in it with an attitude of thanksgiving."
- 1 Thessalonians 5:17 – "Pray without ceasing."

If you want to know how spiritual a person is, take a look at the evidence of time they spend in prayer. Edward McKendree Bounds once said:

> *A prayerless Christian will never learn God's truth; a prayerless ministry will never be able to teach God's truth.*

The Example of George Muller (1805 – 1898)

George Muller became known as a man of prayer because his whole life was centred on prayer. He is recorded as saying that once he was convinced that something was right and that it was for the glory of God he would not give up in prayer for it until the answer came.

The way in which Muller would pray was as follows:

- He took his needs to God.
- He found a promise in the Bible that fitted his need and meditated on that scripture.
- He pleaded with God concerning the scripture promise.

George Muller was devoted to prayer. He prayed continually and was faithful in it. He prayed in the Spirit and he expected an answer.

The following is taken from 'Answers to Prayer, from George Muller's Narratives'.[1]

I seek at the beginning to get my heart into such a state that it has no will of its own in regard to a given matter. Nine-tenths of the difficulties are overcome when our hearts are ready to do the Lord's will, whatever it may be. When one is truly in this state, it is usually but a little way to the knowledge of what His will is.

Having done this, I do not leave the result to feeling or simple impressions. If so, I make myself liable to great delusions.

I seek the will of the Spirit of God through or in connection with the Word of God. The Spirit and the Word must be combined. If I look to the Spirit alone without the Word, I lay myself open to great delusions also.

Next I take into account providential circumstances. These plainly indicate God's will in connection with His Word and Spirit.

I ask God in prayer to reveal His will to me aright.

Thus through prayer to God, the study of the Word and reflection, I come to a deliberate judgment according to the best of my ability and knowledge, and if my mind is thus at peace, and continues so after two or three more petitions, I proceed accordingly. In trivial matters and transactions involving most important issues, I have found this method always effective.

There is much to learn from the way in which George Muller and Smith Wigglesworth were able to reach into the heart of God, but there was another aspect to their lives - that of righteousness before God.

---

[1] Edited by A.E.C Brooks. Printed by The Moody Press.
This is a downloadable free book:
http://manybooks.net/titles/mullerg2589125891-8.html

Prayer and Righteousness

Righteousness is a word that has been a source of debate and confusion for many, so let's take a little time to face this issue head on, in order to find out what God's word has to say.

The word 'righteous' in Hebrew is *tzedek* meaning 'upright, true, straight, innocent, just, and sincere'. It is a state of being right in God's eyes and is also, though not accurately, sometimes called 'rectitude'.

The New Testament actually speaks about two aspects of the word 'righteousness' and it is this that has led some to misunderstanding concerning its true meaning. The two aspects of righteousness are:

- Being made righteous through faith in Jesus.
- Living in obedience to God and in accordance with His gift and word.

RIGHTEOUSNESS – A GIFT OF GOD

The first and most commonly taught meaning of righteousness relates to God's judgement concerning a person's actions. For a person to be righteous, their actions must be pleasing to God, whilst a person deemed unrighteous exhibits ungodly actions that are evil and displeasing to God.

The fact is - no matter how hard we might try - we cannot, of our own effort, attain a state of being right in the eyes of God because we are all sinners.

Romans 3:10

There is none righteous, no, not one.

The judgment is made; we are all guilty in the eyes of God.

Some Bible teachers have stopped at this point, taking this scripture out of context, so that it has become used to interpret the rest of scripture, causing confusion and misunderstanding, spreading tales of hopelessness. Such teaching is wrong. Take a moment to read on to Romans 3:20-31. Here we see plainly that we all fall short of the glory of God, *but* Jesus has redeemed us. He has recovered possession of us. He has paid off our debt by offering himself in pure compensation by his shed blood. The result is that those who in faith accept Jesus as Lord and saviour become united with him; God overlooks the evilness because they are declared righteous, being justified (or vindicated) by Jesus.

This is exactly why no matter whom we are, what we believe, how many good works we may do or how holy others may see us, we are all judged in this sense to be unrighteous until faith in Jesus lifts this huge debt. That is why Jesus is the only way.

John 14:6

Jesus said, "I am the way, and the truth, and the life, no one comes to the Father, but by me."

There is no other way to the kingdom of heaven because there is no other way of paying that debt of sin.

Paul summarises this point:

Romans 5:17

If, because of one man's trespass, death reigned through that one man, much more will those who receive the abundance of grace and the free gift of righteousness reign in life through the one man Jesus Christ.

Righteousness through accepting Jesus by faith is a gift of God. Having been given the gift of righteousness the Christian is expected to live in righteousness.

RIGHTEOUSNESS – ATTAINED THROUGH OBEDIENCE

What evidence is there for saying that there are two aspects to righteousness? If we are going to move forward as Christians, to grow and tap into the power and promises of God, we need to live in God's will, to live in and exercise righteousness and holiness. How? Well, Timothy outlines the source of guidance that we need.

2 Timothy 3:16,17

All scripture is inspired by God and profitable for teaching, for reproof, for correction, and for training in righteousness, that the man of God my be complete for every good work.

The Bible is the Word of God; it teaches, reproves, corrects and trains for the purpose of righteousness. In other words, we can pursue righteousness through right living.

Again we read:

2 Timothy 2:22

So shun youthful passions and aim at righteousness, faith, love, and peace along with those who call upon the Lord from a pure heart.

We are able to "aim at righteousness". In other words, it is something that we can achieve through obedience to, and walking in, the word of God.

It is precisely for these reasons that David was able to confidently express his righteousness before God.

2 Samuel 22:21

The Lord rewarded me according to my righteousness, according to the cleanness of my hands he recompensed me.

This was not a boast of living a sinless life but rather of submission and obedience to God for which a reward is given.

In chapters 1-3, James very neatly helps us to understand that faith and receiving the gift of righteousness must also be evidenced through what Christians think, say and do through their behaviour and actions toward others. The 'actions' or 'works' part of this can be seen in James 2:14-26.

It is plain to see then that receiving the gift of righteousness through faith in Christ does not stop there. We cannot just sit back and carry on as we were; we have a part to play without which we cannot attain answers from God.

Romans 6:12,13

Therefore, do not let sin reign in your mortal body, that you should obey it in its lusts. And do not present your members as instruments of unrighteousness to sin, but present yourself to God as being alive from the dead, and your members as instruments of righteousness to God.

1 Timothy 6:11,12

But as for you, man of God, shun all this, aim at righteousness, godliness, faith, love, steadfastness, gentleness. Fight the good fight of the faith; take hold of the eternal life to which you were called when you made the good confession in the presence of many witnesses.

In short, there is a side to righteousness that requires us to live Holy lives and to keep God's commandments.

If you want to know how to touch the heart of God in prayer it is through righteousness.

- James 5:16 – "The prayer of a righteous man has great power in its effects."
- 1 John 3:22 – "We receive from Him whatever we ask, because we keep His commandments and do what pleases Him."
- 1 Peter 3:12 – "For the eyes of the Lord are upon the righteous, and His ears are open to their prayer."
- Proverbs 15:29 – "The Lord is far from the wicked, but He hears the prayer of the righteous."

The Benefits of Righteous Prayer

Here are just a few of the examples that follow righteous prayers:

Matthew 7:7-12

Ask, and it will be given you; seek, and you will find; knock, and it will be opened to you. For every one who asks receives, and he who seeks finds, and to him who knocks it will be opened. Or what man of you, if his son asks him for bread, will give him a stone? Or if he asks for a fish, wil give him a serpent? If you then, who are evil, know how to give good gifts to your children, how much more will your Father who is in heaven give good things to those who ask him? So whatever you wish that men would do to you, do so to them; for this is the law and the prophets.

Mark 11:24

Therefore I tell you, whatever you ask in prayer, believe that you have received it, and it will be yours.

John 14:13,14

Whatever you ask in my name, I will do it, that the Father may be glorified in the Son; if you ask anything in my name, I will do it.

John 15:7

If you abide in me, and my words abide in you, ask whatever you will, and it shall be done for you.

John 16:23,24

Truly, Truly, I say to you, if you ask anything of the Father, he will give it to you in my name. Hitherto you have asked nothing in my name; ask, and you will receive, that your joy may be full.

Hebrews 4:16

Let us then with confidence draw near to the throne of grace, that we may receive mercy and find grace to help in time of need.

James 5:13-16

Is any one among you suffering? Let him pray. Is any cheerful? Let him sing praise. Is any among you sick? Let him call for the elders of the church, and let him pray over him, anointing him with oil in the name of the Lord; and the prayer of faith will save the sick man, and the Lord will raise him up; and if he has committed sins, he will be forgiven. Therefore, confess your sins to one another, and pray for one another, that you may be healed. The prayer of a righteous man has great power in its effects.

1 John 5:14,15

And this is the confidence which we have in him, that if we ask anything according to his will he hears us. And if we know that he hears us in whatever we ask, we know that we have obtained the requests made of him.

Expect an answer and do not stop until you have it. Miracles are released through both what we say and by doing exactly as God tells us to do. How can we know what God's will is and what we are to do unless we spend time asking, listening for the answer and then doing what God wants us to do?

> *How vast are the possibilities of prayer! How wide is its reach! What great things are accomplished by this divinely appointed means of grace! It lays its hand on Almighty God and moves Him to do what He would not otherwise do if prayer were not offered. It brings things to pass, which would never otherwise occur. The story of prayer is the story of great achievements. Prayer is a wonderful power placed by Almighty God in the hands of His saints, which may be used to accomplish great purposes and to achieve unusual results. Prayer reaches to everything, takes in all things great and small, which are promised by God to the children of men. The only limits to prayer are the promises of God and His ability to fulfil those promises. 'Open thy mouth wide and I will fill it.'*

> - E. M. Bounds -

5. The Language of Healing

The real art of conversation is not only to say the right thing at the right time, but to leave unsaid the wrong thing at the tempting moment.

- Lady Dorothy Nevill (1826-1913) -

Introduction

It may seem odd at first glance, but I am going to concentrate the opening part of this chapter about healing by looking at language. We will consider the type of language that we use, the words that we speak and how these have an impact on our spiritual, mental and physiological reactions as well as the subsequent outcomes that they produce. The reason for this approach is that there is a direct link between the expressions of our inner thoughts, beliefs, faith, spirituality, mental processes and our physiology - each of which, I hope, will become more apparent during the course of this investigation.

In the first part of this chapter we will therefore look at ways in which we can help ourselves to avoid, as far as possible, falling into poor health triggered through use of the negative, errant and damaging language and thinking that distort our beliefs. The poor health that I am speaking of here includes our spiritual health, mental health and physical health. We will also discover in this overview that the exercise of faith and the effectiveness of it depend on what we think and say.

In the second part of the chapter we will investigate how (once a person has become ill with a sickness and healing is needed) healing is open to any and everyone. We will take a look at the biblical healing ministry of the church and its connection with the types of language that we use. This will take us through some difficult questions, and we will consider misleading teachings and doctrines. By the close of the chapter a challenge to revive, or reawaken, God's intended purpose in healing will be given.

Having briefly explained the approach that this chapter will take, I am sure that many will be scratching their heads; this is perhaps an unusual way of tackling the subject of healing. Of course, I fully accept that this is an understandable reaction. The purpose of taking this approach is firstly to write in obedience to what has been laid on my heart and secondly to cover a wide spectrum of positions so that as many people as possible are met at their point of need. It is also very important to grasp and understand that there is a very close link between our mental, physical and spiritual wellbeing, such that dysfunction in any one area can have a knock-on effect on the other areas. This is something that is all too frequently left out of discussions on this topic, except in the medical and psychological fields of study.

In writing about healing I am acutely aware that this rich blessing from God has also been a point of misunderstanding, confusion, hurt and a stumbling block for some. I am sure that we can all point to scriptures that positively say that the sick will recover and yet in our personal experiences we will know of those for whom this simply has not been the case; some have even died. Satan has had a field day with the havoc that he has created. From the outset, therefore, let us consider the following facts:

- Sickness, infirmity, disease, oppression and demon possession come from Satan.
- Disobedience, pride and sinful wilfulness are the domain in which we have been born. Dysfunction of our thinking, beliefs and actions has a direct impact on our mental, physical and spiritual wellbeing. We can create illness in our own bodies by upsetting the normal balances of our make-up.
- Neither God nor Jesus condemns the world; rather they have demonstrated love and compassion to incomprehensible levels.
- Jesus came into the world to destroy the works of Satan such as those described above. That is why he brought good news of the kingdom of God as well as prevailing over sicknesses and demon possession.
- To point the finger at God and blame Him for all the ills and bad things that happen in the world and in our lives is to unjustly deny His sovereignty, to disallow Him to work as He would really want, and to hand control to the work of Satan.

This is not said or intended in any judgmental way, but is there a position that we should adopt before we go running to blame God or to find excuses for God? Should the first and honest place to look be at the evil that surrounds us and also at our own thoughts, actions and behaviours? God has given to each of us a free will, and He will not deny us this gift of freedom. We can hold firm to our position, to our actions and wilfulness, or we can humble ourselves and hand our free will to God. The choice is freely ours individually to make, but in having a choice we must surely also accept responsibility for our actions before casting blame elsewhere.

It is important from the outset to clarify that I will not analyze historical events in order to determine how the church has lost its way in these matters; rather I am addressing a decline in our spiritual and relational walk with God that has lead to dysfunctions in our Christian living. The ground upon which the foundations of this chapter has been laid and built is that the Bible is the word of God and that God is wholly truthful in what He says and promises. My belief is that God's word has not changed over time and that His promises are as relevant and vibrant in today's church and the Christian's life as they have always been.

During the course of the ministry of Jesus and the foundations of the New Testament church we read over and over again that healings took place and that these accompanied the gospel proclamation, being witnesses to God's almighty power and love. The reason why I say this is because one of the signs that followed Jesus and his disciples was that all were healed. For example:

Luke 6:19, emphasis added
And all the crowd sought to touch [Jesus], for power came forth from him and healed them _all_.

And again:

Acts 5:16, emphasis added
The people also gathered from the towns around Jerusalem, bringing the sick and those afflicted with unclean spirits, and they were _all_ healed.

There are many, many other references to show that *all* those who came to Jesus or his disciples seeking healing were healed. This fact is something that has unfortunately been lost in time and is sadly not the experience of the Christian church today because it has drifted away from the power of God. In its place we have watered down the scriptures.

Now, having made the statement that all were healed, what often follows from sceptics are strong objections in which examples of the 'missing' power of God are given and the word of God is watered down in order to explain matters that are not understood.

For example, some immediately point to the disciples who were unable to heal the epileptic boy in Mark 9:14-29 and exclaim for all who will listen that this is proof that healing does not always take place. The first point to correct in this flawed challenge is that the boy *was* healed; therefore to suggest otherwise is actually untrue. The second point that we do well to take note of is that of the words of Jesus:

Mark 9:19

O faithless generation, how long am I to be with you?

Healing was being sought from faithless hearts. The tools were available to the disciples as much as they are to us today but the question is, do we trust God enough to use them? The third point is seen in verses 28 and 29:

Mark 9:28-29

And when he had entered the house, his disciples asked him privately, 'Why could we not cast it out?' And he said to them, 'This kind cannot be driven out by anything but prayer.'

The disciples were in their learning stages and Jesus was teaching them about discipleship, prayer and healing, where some healings are connected to evil spirit possession amongst other reasons.

Another challenge to healing comes when people say that healing does not always work and point to Jesus himself who attempted to heal a blind man near Bethsaida. First we read that Jesus spat on the man's eyes and laid his hands on him. When asked by Jesus, "Do you see anything?"

(Mark 8:23) the man replied, "I see men, but they look like trees walking." Stopping here, the claim is made that healing does not always take place. However, reading on we discover that Jesus then again laid hands on the man and his sight was fully restored. The man was healed. He had been blind, unable to see anything, but he left Jesus totally healed. How can one suggest that this healing was not manifested?

The Bible is clear in its statement that all will be healed but, as the American evangelist Fred Francis Bosworth (1877-1958) noted:

> *The greatest barrier to the faith of many seeking bodily healing in our day is the uncertainty in their minds as to it being the will of God to heal all. Nearly everyone knows that God does heal some, but there is much in modern theology that keeps people from knowing what the Bible clearly teaches — that healing is provided for all. It is impossible to boldly claim, by faith, a blessing that we are not sure God offers. The power of God can be claimed only where the will of God is known.*

Over time the church has lost its relationship and power connection with God to the point where it simply does not know God. The resulting experience of Christians and inadequate teaching have limited our belief in God's will to heal. Therefore our language (what we say about healing) does not reflect 'healing faith'. In order to explain gaps in our understanding, we try to find man-created, plausible explanations, instead of going back to what God's word actually says and maintaining faith in this. The result is dysfunction, a deepening loss of personal contact with God and a weakening of faith; even our prayer language has become faithlessly apologetic and our expectations half-hearted. Coupled with all of this are the damaging influences of following tradition, humanism and, of course, sin.

Dear friends, this is not a time to remain silent but rather to speak out that we need to get back to New Testament church basics. There is absolutely no reason at all why we should accept failures in people being healed. Unfortunately, we rejoice prematurely over those that are healed whilst we do not spiritually weep to the core of our soul for the many that are not healed. Now please do not misunderstand me; it is of course right that we praise God with thankful hearts for those that are healed. But are

137

we equally mindful of those that are not healed in our churches and daily lives? What I am saying is that no one who comes for healing should go away or be left in any other way than totally healed. To fail even one person in the healing ministry is a travesty of Christian living and faith in God. It is a tragedy that Christians in the church are not healed and some have needlessly died because of neglect in teachings concerning God's healing promises. I am, of course, as already stated, aware that this statement is not in line with our general experiences, but what we have experienced is not something we can rely upon; we can rely upon God's word. The Psalmist encourages us in the promises of God saying:

Psalm 103:3-5

Bless the Lord, O my soul, and forget not all his benefits, who forgives all your iniquity, who heals all your diseases, who redeems your life from the pit, who crowns you with steadfast love and mercy, who satisfies you with good as long as you live so that your youth is renewed like the eagle's.

If healing does not take place then we must do what the disciples did - humble ourselves and ask why; what is it that we are not doing?

- Is it our lack of faith?
- Is it our lack of prayer commitment?
- Is it our failure to seek God's guidance as to what and how we should act?
- Is it to do with what we say and think?

Prudence in our Speech

The opening quotation by Lady Dorothy Nevill may have surprised or even taken some of you aback as you asked, "What has that to do with healing?" I am not trying to align with Lady Dorothy other than to say that actually the words we use can heal and soothe or they can injure and leave deep hurts. What deep hurts have we left for those who have sought God in healing? We also learn from Ecclesiastes 3:7 that prudence in what we say, or do not say, is important, and we read that there is "a time to keep silence and a time to speak". It is precisely because of this prudence and guarding of what we say (or what causes us to say what we say) that this chapter leads us to focus our attention on the type of language that we use concerning healing:

- What we think and say about healing.
- The way in which our beliefs, thoughts, speech and actions (based on our understanding of healing) make us who we are and either open or keep closed channels to God's power.

God's word does not support lacks or failures in exercising faith and healing, so why do we accept anything less and speak anything less?

The words that we speak have the power to destroy, to bring hate, to cause strife and wars, to injure and cause illness, to prevent healing and to separate us from God. Alternatively they can bring soothing to another person, they can lift and encourage, they can bring love and unity, they can lift us from despondency, they can activate healing and the power of God. If we are unable to speak faith and God's word in healing it is best that we remain silent. If we are able to speak faith and act in faith then let us speak out and exercise what we say in action.

The fact is, if we change our words from negativity to positivity, if we change from disbelief to belief, then we change our world and we change our relationship with God and with one another. Words have the power to totally change our lives for better or for worse. The sad part of this is that none of this is new - it is not something that you and I are unaware of, but it is something that most people have failed to tap into and act upon in daily living. The question is, of course, why? We will explore this in more detail later, but basically it is because words affect our emotions. They activate our memory of good and bad experiences and feelings. They go to the very core of our being. They stir what truly lies deep within our hearts and souls - the real people that we are, the real thoughts and beliefs that we hold. Writing to the church in Corinth, Paul, speaking of repentance, poses for us a worthwhile challenge:

2 Corinthians 13:5

Examine yourselves, to see whether you are holding to your faith. Test yourselves. Do you not realise that Jesus Christ is in you? – unless indeed you fail to meet the test!

Have you ever wondered why some prayers are not answered even though the Bible makes incredible claims and promises? In Mark, we find these powerful words spoken by Jesus himself who states clearly and emphatically that they are absolutely true:

Mark 11:22-25

And Jesus answered them, 'Have faith in God. Truly, I say to you, whoever says to this mountain, 'Be taken up and cast into the sea,' and does not doubt in his heart, but believes that what he says will come to pass, it will be done for him. Therefore I tell you, whatever you ask in prayer, believe that you have received it, and it will be yours. And whenever you stand praying, forgive, if you have anything against any one; so that your Father also who is in heaven may forgive you your trespasses.'

These are not 'pie in the sky' statements. Jesus said, "Truly, I say to you" or, in our modern terms, "I am telling you a fact."

Let's take a moment to look again at these verses and examine closely what these amazing words spoken by Jesus actually say. Did you notice how many times in these four verses Jesus used words such as 'say', 'tell' and 'ask'? That which is *spoken* produces the power associated with the statements. Take another look at these verses with the key words highlighted:

Mark 11:22-25, emphasis added

And Jesus answered them, 'Have faith in God. Truly, I <u>say</u> to you, whoever <u>says</u> to this mountain, 'Be taken up and cast into the sea,' and does not doubt in his heart, but believes that what he <u>says</u> will come to pass, it will be done for him. Therefore I <u>tell</u> you, whatever you <u>ask</u> in prayer, believe that you have received it, and it will be yours. And whenever you stand praying, forgive, if you have anything against any one; so that your Father also who is in heaven may forgive you your trespasses.

We discover here three keys:

- We need to have faith in God - not only to know that He will answer but also to have an assured conviction in our hearts, without wavering. We need to know and trust that God is truthful in what He says.

- We need to speak out, or confess with our tongue, our faith and trust in God in order to release power beyond measure. Words, whether thought, spoken or written are our way of communicating what lies deep within our hearts. James outlines the power of the tongue in chapter 3:1-12, speaking of it as a powerful tool with which we both bless and curse. If we can bridle the tongue we gain control of our lives and tap into untold, God-given power. If we do not bridle the tongue we release power but it is not of God; it is dysfunctional and potentially destructive.
- We need to voice forgiveness so that God can forgive us. Unforgiveness blocks forgiveness; it separates and brings disharmony.

1 Peter 3:9-12

Do not return evil for evil or reviling for reviling; but on the contrary bless, for to this you have been called, that you may obtain a blessing. For, 'He that would love life and see good days, let him keep his tongue from evil and his lips from speaking guile; let him turn away from evil and do right; let him seek peace and pursue it. For the eyes of the Lord are upon the righteous, and his ears are open to their prayer. But the face of the Lord is against those that do evil.'

Guarding our tongue and being a blessing is what we are called to do. If you want to get God to take notice and touch His heart, take a look again at what this scripture says. The eyes of the Lord are upon the righteous and His ears are open to the prayers of the righteous who pray in faith and total confidence that God is true to His word. God hears the prayers prayed by the righteous in faith and He will answer. Accepting or expecting anything less than healing when we ask for it is not exercising faith.

The Christian walk, healing and the power of God are released through what we think, say and ultimately do. It is worth spending a little time to understand these golden nuggets of truth and why the words that we think and speak out are so powerful. This understanding is necessary before considering God's purpose and will in healing because healing is inextricably linked to thoughts, words and beliefs.

PART ONE

The Power of Words

It is very important that we first grasp the immensity and power of words and what lies behind the meaning that they convey both to the sender and to the person who receives them (in written or spoken form). Once received, words can draw out from within us emotional responses that may control or influence our thoughts and subsequent behaviour. No matter who we are, words spoken and heard (or written and read) have an effect upon us as receivers. Once they have been communicated and received the senders cannot take them back.

It is truly amazing, if you think about it, that although communication is a necessary part of survival and daily living for us as human beings, it is one of the most difficult and potentially misunderstood areas of our lives as well as a cause of conflict. How amazing that we can be so inept! Oh, how many times I have said something that was received in a totally different way from that in which it was meant or intended! How many times I have anguished and carefully thought through how to communicate a given explanation, and it has been received with the opposite effect! Much of this relates not only to our own communication blunders but also to the receiver's cultural, emotional, situational context and personal belief filters, making communication a complex and challenging task.

In order to grasp the enormity of what I am saying let's consider this in another way. The words that we speak, write or think create impressions, images and expectations derived from what we have previously learned and experienced throughout our lives. In psychological terms they build connections in our brain which influence both how we think and what we think. They can affect our physiology and subsequent actions and reactions. It is worth stressing that because our thoughts are linked closely to our physiology and actions, a very powerful connection is made between the words we use and the consequential outcomes; the words manifest themselves in sickness or, as the psychologist may phrase it, psychosomatic responses.

In the published collection of dialect and folk phrases entitled 'Folk Phrases of Four Counties'[2] we find reference to a very well known children's nursery rhyme, which says:

Sticks and stones can break my bones, but words [names] can never hurt me.

The sentiment claimed by the author of this rhyme is that whilst a physical assault on a person will hurt physically, the cruelty of words or that of name-calling does not hurt or bother them.

You may perhaps, as an outsider looking down on this situation and having no direct involvement, initially feel that this is a nice and true sentiment; but, oh dear, many can testify how utterly untrue and wrong this is. Just look at the misery caused by the words and taunts so often lavished in the workplace or in schools where the recipient's life is made a misery. How many times have we heard of people for whom the psychological effects of words have caused them to take their own life?

Because words are so tightly and intricately linked with our emotions, the decisions that we make and the actions that we take can be influenced by words even though there may be no truth or logic behind them; the actions may not be beneficial to us personally but they benefit others at our expense.

Our emotional states are changeable and to a greater or lesser extent our decisions *can* be affected - especially in emotionally charged situations and environments and through the compelling arguments that a person may use.

To illustrate this point, recent research suggests that as little as 5% can influence 95% of a crowd. We have probably all been caught up in situations where we have been swept along with the crowd whether in music festivals, the theatre, churches, rallies or even at market traders and sales pitches. Have you ever started to jump up and down, waving your arms, shouting out or crying in a crowd when normally this would not be your behaviour? Have you ever found yourself accepting what someone is saying or purchasing an item in a sales pitch and later wondering why you had gone along with the idea? Research following riot situations has found

---

[2] G. F. Northall (1894)

that people have started to act in a way that was far from their normal behaviour. Some have even reported stealing items that they did not need or want simply because others were stealing.

In these circumstances we may find ourselves making choices that are actually those of another person. It is always a good idea to walk away and take time out of the emotionally charged setting, as well as to check the validity of what has been said. This is true regardless of what is spoken or written about and is particularly important with subjects such as healing. The emotional states that can be attached to healing are so fragile and sensitive that they deserve respect. I have no wish to be unnecessarily controversial, and I am certainly not making criticisms of healing ministries across the globe. Please understand that I only wish to look at what the Bible has to say; therefore I invite you to take a fresh look at how Jesus conducted healings.

Why Are Words So Powerful?

The power of words is derived from three interconnected aspects of who we are: our psychological and physiological make-up (which are totally inseparable) and, underpinning these, our spiritual make-up which has been made dysfunctional as a result of sin. In order to understand these better we will revisit some of the points made previously. We will refocus our attention on the fact that words have power because the words trigger meanings and connections that we individually attach to them, which in turn trigger emotions and feelings. They bring into focus previous experiences and memories that lie deep within our unconscious mind, and they activate our beliefs and subsequent behavioural responses. It is for these reasons that different people react in different ways to the same words and situations. Intonation in our speech adds impact to the words spoken as well as how they are received and perceived through our individual language filters, guarded by the beliefs that we hold. The words that we think and speak have an autonomic impact upon our physiology, which simply responds as it is commanded to do by the brain. It follows therefore that positive thoughts produce positive feelings and reactions so that normal body functioning can be maintained. Negative thoughts, on the other hand, produce negative feelings and responses in the body and the body systems function in a disrupted manner, leading to breakdown of normal chemical flows and body organ function. Sin and separation from God have a negative effect, and the further we choose to walk from God the greater the potential for disharmony. The words that we speak and write also have an impact on those that receive them powerful enough to change lives! Unfortunately most of this power is at worse negatively and harmfully used and at best underused. In short, this is how we are made and wired. We have far more power at our fingertips than we often realise.

The words of Genesis 1:26 provide for us an insight into our spiritual link and why we are made and wired in the way that we are. We read God saying, "Let us make man in our image, after our likeness." In making us in His image (that is *all* of us, no matter who we are) God passed on certain qualities that have remained in us, manifesting themselves in the power behind our words and the strength of what we believe. It is because of this God-given ability that positive thinking, positive beliefs and positive speaking can all produce positive results, including healing. These abilities are not solely in the realm of the Christian believer. If you do not believe me just look around you and see for yourself the positive and powerful qualities of famous people, entrepreneurs, sportspeople and those that recover from serious illness through use of positive thoughts and language, even though they may not have a belief in, or commitment to, God. Unfortunately sin has brought malfunctioning and disharmony that disrupt our thoughts, words, deeds and beliefs so that our words and beliefs often carry sinful and harmful forces that impact our spiritual and physical health and wellbeing. God does not wish this upon us, and so He gave up what was most precious to Him - His only son. Through Jesus much of this, if not all, can be restored.

You may of course ask, "So what need is there of God if we already have the potential to exercise power through what we think and say?" This is a logical question, being one that lies at the root of sin itself for many want to take control and follow their sinful nature. The fact is that sin, resulting from the fall of Adam, has separated us from God - rather like taking a plug out of a socket to disconnect an appliance - and it has disrupted both our relationship with God and also our power connection. Those without God cannot use positive thinking or positive beliefs to enter the kingdom of heaven. This can only be restored (like the plug being reconnected to the socket) through what Jesus did on the cross to pay for our sins. They cannot of themselves tap into the power of God and raise the dead or see God-given signs, wonders and miracles.

I have long been intrigued by the story of Moses and Aaron found in Exodus chapters seven through to fourteen. They were sent by God to speak with Pharaoh and we read in these Exodus accounts about a series of miracles that God performed through Moses and Aaron in order to touch the heart of Pharaoh to release God's people. However, Pharaoh called upon wise men, sorcerers and magicians who used their secret arts and were able to mimic many of the same things; so Pharaoh was not persuaded. As we read on, however, we discover that these wise men, sorcerers and magicians had limited abilities; they could not perform miracles to the level of those that Moses and Aaron performed. What they achieved was within their limitations, and what they were able to pass on to others was no more than self, sin and often deceit. The Christian, on the other hand, exercising faith through holy living, is open to all that God has to offer and able to pass on 'life and truth' evidence and messages of God Himself because of what Jesus accomplished on the cross.

Paul outlines the impact that Adam and Jesus have upon us in the following words:

1 Corinthians 15:21,22

For as by a man came death, by a man has come also the resurrection of the dead. For as in Adam all die, so also in Christ shall all be made alive.

Taking this theme further, we discover Paul writing to the church in Ephesus calling for the people to restore their lives:

Ephesians 4:22-24

Put off your old nature which belongs to your former manner of life and is corrupt through deceitful lusts, and be renewed in the spirit of your minds, and put on the new nature, created after the likeness of God in true righteousness and holiness.

The amazing truth is, we are able to restore the power of our words that God originally intended for us through faith in Him. The sad part of this is that most Christians have failed to restore the power that God wishes for us all because they are not completely connected to Him by faith. What I mean here, using the electric analogy, is that the plug is connected but a fault in the wiring exists - the wiring being faith and prayer. Most of our connection is intermittent because faith is lacking (Mark 11:22 – "Have faith in God") and continual contact through prayer is missing (1 Thessalonians 5:17 – "Pray constantly").

Throughout the Bible, and particularly in the New Testament, we read over and over again about having faith, guarding our speech, renewing our minds, spending time talking with God in prayer and living righteous and holy lives. Repeatedly we read that whatever we ask, we will receive; what we say, we will receive; having faith pleases God; and so on. What we say, the language that we use and what we think are key to being human and in the likeness of God.

The power of words goes beyond our comprehension. God spoke and it happened. Take a look at Genesis chapter one and note how many times we read that "God spoke and it was so."

- Verse 3 – "And God said, 'Let there be light' and there was light."
- Verse 6 – "And God said, 'Let there be a firmament.'"
- Verse 9 – "And God said, 'Let the waters under the heavens be gathered.'"
- Verse 11 – "God said, 'Let the earth put forth vegetation.'"
- Verse 14 – "And God said, 'Let there be lights.'"
- Verse 20 – "And God said, 'Let the waters bring forth swarms of living creatures.'"
- Verse 24 – "And God said, 'Let the earth bring forth living creatures.'"
- Verse 26 – "Then God said, 'Let us make man in our image, after our likeness.'"

The efficacy of God's word is clearly stated and outlined for us in the words of Isaiah:

Isaiah 55:10,11

For as the rain and snow come down from heaven, and return not thither but water the earth, making it bring forth and sprout, giving seed to the sower and bread to the eater; so shall my word be that goes forth from my mouth; it shall not return to me empty, but it shall accomplish that which I purpose, and prosper in the thing for which I sent it.

As we speak, we too can tap into the power of God and, as it says in Mark 11:23, "move mountains".

Words Reflect Who We Are

The words that we use are a reflection of the inner person - the real person that we are - and this in turn reflects the way in which we behave. Our attitudes and personality are revealed through the way in which we speak to, and treat, others.

Matthew 15:18

What comes out of the mouth proceeds from the heart.

Most of the time we do not actually know ourselves (that is, the *real* us.) We do not take time out to listen to ourselves. We speak without thinking about the consequences and the impact that our words will have upon others, whether for good or for bad. We do not realise what a forceful effect our words may have upon others and how they can influence them.

When I was in my early teenage years I was speaking with a group of friends which included an attractive and sport-loving, fit young lady. There was a great deal of banter going on with one thing leading to another, and jokingly I uttered (I do not know why), "You should go on a diet." For one reason or another I never saw this girl again, but I discovered through a friend some time later that not only had I missed the point that this lovely young lady was really fond of me but that she had gone on a diet even though there was no physical or any other reason for her to do so! Those careless words had a profound effect upon this lovely young lady who cared about and wanted to please me.

I do not know what lasting affect my stupidity may have had on this young lady. Certainly the effect upon me has not only lasted over many years but has also left me in utter disbelief regarding my clumsy thoughtlessness. I deeply regret those words for which I am ashamed and sought forgiveness. Of course, perhaps worse still is when we calculate and deliberately use words to hurt or manipulate or even to dominate others but neither scenario is one to be proudly associated with.

Our words have the power to:

- Care or to hurt
- Encourage or discourage
- Love or hate
- Build or destroy
- Make or break

Words can also be a two-edged sword because, as I have already suggested, they not only have an effect on others but can also rebound and have an effect upon our belief systems and even our own physiology.

Our beliefs are formed from the time that we are born and they develop as we go through life experiences being confirmed through what people say, our self-talk, through rewards and punishment systems and so on. We form our own perceptions and we become what we think. As parents, what we say to our children can have a lasting imprint, affecting how they conduct themselves in years to come. Parenting is an awesome responsibility, one that I am sorry to have failed to realise and act upon. Thank goodness, however, that there are examples of savvy parenting.

It is important to encourage children not only in their performance but also in their character. Take a look at these examples:

- "I saw the way in which you held your tongue in that situation. Well done!"
- "I see from your actions that you are kind. That was a lovely thing you did."
- "You did not do that well but I think that you can do better."

If on occasion we get cross with our children and tell them off, it is also important to show the way of forgiveness, to get to the child's level and say, "I am sorry. You are too valuable to be spoken to like that. Will you forgive me?" I am not advocating that we do not discipline. I am simply saying that there are right ways of doing it; if we get it wrong, we can lead the way to forgiveness.

These are principles that we can take into the workplace and into our social settings and church life.

If you take time to listen to conversations or even to your own speech, they will not only reveal the absurdities of our language but also how we reflect our inner thoughts and how these words and thoughts have an effect upon us. Take a look at the following examples:

- "You are a pain in the neck."
- "You make me sick."
- "You tickle me to death."
- "Nothing good ever happens to me."
- "You never do anything."
- "You make me mad."
- "I am too old."
- "I am so fat."

Now take a moment to really think seriously about the impact of these absurd words, what they are saying about the person who has spoken them and how they reflect what is going on in that person.

You may say that these are just expressions of speech - they do not mean anything. If they do not mean anything, why are they being used? What effect are they having?

I once 'joked' that my six-pack was becoming a barrel. My barrel is no joke! What we say, if we say it often enough, can become what we think, how we act, who we become and what happens to us.

Let's consider two true stories from my own experience.

THE STORY OF WILF

I first met Wilf, a happy-go-lucky type of person, when he came to carry out some work at my house. Wilf was a lovely man who, as well as being exceedingly good at his job, had many interesting stories to relate. Although you would not have been able to tell, seeing him nimbly climbing up and down ladders, he had unfortunately suffered several heart attacks, which I only discovered when a trench needed to be dug through the heavy clay of my garden. He was willing to do the dig, but he said that it might take him a while. Needless to say, I dug the trench!

About a year later I asked Wilf to do some further work, so he came one sunny Sunday afternoon to view the job. Over a cup of tea in the back garden the conversation turned to pensions. Wilf declared that "with one thing and another" he would need to live to seventy-five to begin to make his contributions back; he wondered if at the age of sixty-one it was worth continuing to pay extra contributions. He then said, "Of course, I will not make seventy-five," and added that his daughter had said he would die in his sleep. I was alarmed by his frank statement and said to him that he should not speak and think that way.

Wilf returned at 8am the next morning with his usual cheerful smile and completed the job by coffee time. I asked how much I owed him and promised to take the money to him first thing on the Tuesday morning. With a smile he replied, "You worry too much. You are not running away!" and with that gave a smile, a wave and drove off.

First thing on the Tuesday, I determined to get to the bank, and I walked to Wilf's house to make payment as promised. Knocking on the door I was greeted by Wilf's son-in-law and I asked if I could speak with Wilf. My request was greeted with, "He died in his sleep last night."

THE STORY OF MY DAD

My father, a man that I loved deeply, was a survivor of the forced and hard labour Gulags in Siberia during the early 1940's where average temperatures fell to -21°C and, according to some reports, even reaching -55°C. I remember when I was a youngster and my father (aged 55, a man of both physical and mental strength) moved concrete posts approximately seven feet long. We began by taking one end each, but to speed things up my father hoisted one concrete post over his shoulder as if lifting a light-weighted tube and smartly walked off. I did not wish to be outdone so I too grabbed a post while he was not looking and managed to get it across my shoulder. I can remember to this day the pain as the post dug into my shoulder.

I watched with astonishment as my father, seeing my efforts, proceeded to lift *two* concrete posts, one over each shoulder, and smartly marched off. Needless to say, I could not be outdone even if it was hurting. When he came to lifting three posts I gave in!

Even more astonishing (and I cannot to this day explain or imagine how) my father, aged about seventy, lifted his garden shed on his own and placed four old wooden reclaimed oak railway sleepers (which weigh in the region of 180lbs each) under the shed in order to raise it up. He was a man who did not see a problem; he saw a need and found a way to meet that need.

After his untimely death of a stroke I discovered that my father had often said, although never in my hearing, that he would survive until he was 72. He died in his 73rd year - four months after his 72nd birthday - a fit, active and strong man.

I cannot prove that either of these men had died as a result of their self-talk, but I can tell you that they got what they had said.

The Mind–Body Connection

Try this simple exercise experiment.

In a quiet room, sit still and remain very quiet for a few moments. Breathe slowly and deeply, relaxing the shoulders, neck and arms. When you are ready, cast your mind back to a time when you felt lethargic, tired and just not wanting to get up or do anything. Your limbs and body felt weak. Try to recall as much detail about this time as you can - what it was like, what you heard, what you could smell, what you could see and so on. As you begin to experience these physical feelings, think also about your emotional feelings of sadness and tiredness. Hold these thoughts and feelings for twenty to thirty seconds. Now try to stand up. Take careful note of what you experience.

Having done this exercise and recorded your experiences sit down again and relax in the same way as before. This time think of a time when you were in the opposite situation. You felt lively, energetic, and strong, you wanted to get up and be really active. Every part of your body felt alive and vibrant. Try to recall as much detail as you can - what it was like, what you heard, what you could smell, what you could see and so on. As you begin to experience these physical feelings, think about your emotions, feelings of happiness, excitement and power. Hold these thought and feelings for twenty seconds or more. Now stand up.

Compare the two experiences as you stood up. In the first experience you may have found difficulty in standing, your body feeling heavy, your shoulders dropped and head down. You did not feel particularly pleasant. In the second you may have jumped up; you stood tall and were ready for action.

This simple experiment can demonstrate the link between our minds and our bodies and the way in which our thoughts can significantly affect our performance. It crudely but effectively demonstrates that our bodies respond to our thoughts and feelings.

In many ways it should come as no surprise to us that our brains and what we think are closely linked to our body, muscles and function of the cells etc, leading to the actions that we take and our general health. If there is a dysfunction in our thoughts this will be evident in some way in our bodies. For example, if we are under stress our normal body chemical flow will be affected so that tension can lead to muscular pain as fibres contract. Other symptoms such as high blood pressure, being unable to sleep and so on manifest themselves as a result of the unity between the brain, mind and body chemistry.

Throughout our lives, neural networks of the brain develop in response to learning experiences and stimuli. Neurons not only interlink with other neurons; they also connect with skeletal muscles at what is known as the neuromuscular junction. Here the brain uses the chemical acetylcholine, a neurotransmitter for memory and attention which communicates with muscles. Dopamine, another of the brain's chemical messengers, helps to regulate what is called 'fine motor movement'.

Put simply, our emotions generate physical responses. For example, if we listen to an eerie story the words and tones used can make us feel on edge or send a shiver up our spines. If a sudden noise is sounded we might jump or scream. What has happened is that the negative suggestion has produced a fear emotion which has a physical response of shaking, a shiver up our spine and maybe even a cold sweat. In the same way that negative language or images create negative emotional reactions, positive language and images produce positive reactions. Our psychological state has a direct impact on chemicals released in the body. Fear produces adrenaline, the 'fight or flight' response, which raises blood pressure etc and lowers the immune system. Positive thought and happiness chemicals such as serotonin or endorphins can boost the immune system.

Psychosomatic Illness

Let's begin by looking at the meaning of the word 'psychosomatic'. The word is taken from the Greek words *psyche* meaning 'mind' and *somatic* meaning 'body' or 'physical'. In medical terms psychosomatic is associated with disorders that have physical symptoms originating from mental or emotional causes. In other words, it is the influence of the mind on the body and the body on the mind.

Hysteria

Until the twentieth century, what we now refer to as psychosomatic disorder was originally called hysteria. Finding its original root in the Greek word *hustera* meaning 'uterus', Hippocrates used its medical term *hysterikos*. It was a diagnostic label referring to a certain state of the mind, particularly excess of fear and emotion, being often originally associated with women.

If we go back to the Middle Ages we come across two Persian physicians called Abu Zayd al-Balkhi and Ali ibn Abbas al-Majusi who pioneered psychophysiology and psychosomatic medicine. Abbas al-Majusi is quoted as saying:

Joy and contentment can bring a better living status to many who would otherwise be sick and miserable due to unnecessary sadness, fear, worry and anxiety.

In this quote we have some powerful statements linking physical outcomes of sickness with psychological states such as misery, fear, worry and anxiety.

By the 1840's hysteria had become a serious medical subject. Interest in psychosomatic illness and the mind-body link grew rapidly during the 1930's-1960's. Although there is no consensus, it is said by various medical experts that between 70% and 90% of health problems today are psychosomatically connected.

In the medical world it is recognised that there are four main causes of illness:

- Trauma – For example, a broken bone or head injury from a blow that can also lead to a change in the body's functioning.
- Toxicity – Sources of toxicity are, for example, radiation, drugs, chemicals (for example those found in some beauty or hair products), food additives and pollution etc. These can upset the nervous system and normal cell and chemical balances of the body
- Transmission – This includes those illnesses, or the propensity toward illness, that may be passed on genetically
- Thoughts – The thoughts, language and speech that we use have the power to alter the chemical balance of our various body systems. The cells, tissues and organs of our body respond to the messages that they receive, by means of receptors (specialized proteins that have specific responses to specific chemical messages). They are not able to distinguish between what is right and what is wrong! They are not able to question the message that they receive; so if we constantly send negative signals, the outcome will also be negative.

It makes sense also that if the messages and signals that our body systems receive are 'good' then the body will respond in health. Indeed God has made us so that our bodies, when functioning correctly, protect us from illness, and we also have an amazing capacity to heal ourselves.

There is growing research evidence to suggest that it is possible to speed injury recovery through use of mental skills and techniques such as imagery, self-talk and hypnosis. Thought patterns through meditation and progressive muscle relaxation techniques are able to relax the body and give 'time out' from the pressures of daily life.

The Message

What we hear, read and learn can have a direct effect on what we believe; what we believe can have a direct effect on what we think; what we think can have a direct effect on what we say; and, in turn, what we say can have a direct effect on our health.

To live life is to face various forms of stress. It is not the stress itself but how we deal with it that can create problems. Stress is born from pressures that we cannot cope with or do not know how to handle. It can also arise from involving ourselves in things that we know deep down are wrong, causing inner conflict.

The stress response is a natural process through which the body tries to protect us. Beyond a certain level, stress responses cease to be helpful and begin to damage us. Psychologically the body is not able to make distinctions between stress causes such as overwork, arguments, financial problems and so on. The more that stress is activated the more our body systems are upset. If the body does not get respite it begins to destroy itself as worry and anxiety set in.

Jesus says:

Matthew 11:28-30

Come to me all who are weary and heavy-laden, and I will give you rest. Take my yoke upon you and learn from me, for I am gentle and humble in heart; and you shall find rest for your souls for my yoke is easy and my load is light.

Take a closer look at this verse. All too often the first sentence is used in isolation from the remainder of the text, losing its impact. We can offload our stresses. It is a personal choice requiring the personal action of changing our emphasis and how we look at our problems. In biblical terms it means turning our attention to, and meditating upon, God. Here we have a role model as we learn how Jesus lived His life.

A Warning Reminder

The roots or basis from which we speak and the effect of our language - what we say and how we say it - are manifested in the reactions that we receive from others, the impact that we have and also through our own body health. We may perhaps not need to have further confirmation, but as if to press these points home we come across the following plain-speaking statement made by Jesus:

Matthew 12:34-37

You brood of vipers, how can you, being evil, speak what is good? For the mouth speaks out of that which fills the heart. The good man out of his good treasure brings forth what is good; and the evil man out of his evil treasure brings forth what is evil. And I say to you that every careless word that men shall speak, they shall render account for it in the Day of Judgment. For by your words you shall be justified and by your words you shall be condemned.

The language and speech that we use, whether as an outward expression or an inward dialogue, is *our own choice*. I am not trying to claim perfection; I simply want to remind myself that it is my responsibility to change and it is also my responsibility to react with positivity to claim a health-filled lifestyle.

The Story of Graham Miles

Following a stroke, Graham Miles suffered from Locked-in Syndrome, being aware of what was going on around him but unable to move apart from his eyelids - hardly even able to breathe.

Doctors told him that he would be a prisoner of his own body, unable to speak or to move and that he would never recover.

Graham made a decision: he was going to prove the doctors were wrong. His thoughts were focussed upon his recovery. He quickly realised that the first thing that he needed to do was to concentrate his thoughts on the paralysis of his chest so that he could breathe properly. In particular, Graham realised that his thinking had to be concentrated on his diaphragm. After a couple of months, movement of the diaphragm and chest began and the initial breakthrough achieved. From there Graham went on from to walk with the aid of sticks, speak and pass his driving test. Incredibly, Graham makes one statement that may limit his progress; he says, "I will never be fully recovered."

Let us be thankful to God that the majority of us we will not have to face this battle in our lives in order to demonstrate the power of the mind. Many of us, however, have an unseen battle raging - that of negative language and thinking - that can affect our health and the health of others. It is important to surround ourselves with positive reading, positive people and positive thinking opportunities based upon the Word of God and a relationship with Him.

PART TWO

In Need of Healing

Let us take a closer look at the subject of healing. There are many people who are totally unaware of both the impact and power of what they believe, think and speak. In thinking and writing about healing one cannot fail to become aware of how negativity affects health and how faith can break down healing barriers.

As we have discovered already, negative thinking has led to a wide range of psychosomatic illnesses; this together with traumas, disease and toxins provide many reasons why people need to seek help from one or more healing source. Sometimes the healing requirements become what we term 'miracle needs' - that is, when all other avenues have failed or medicines are unable to help.

We have talked a lot about the power of words and so it should come as no surprise that the Bible, the Word of God, is widely recognised as containing power. As mentioned previously, Smith Wigglesworth once said that he had read no other book than the Bible. His thoughts and speech were centred on what the Bible had to say, and he became known as a man of faith as a result of the many examples of faith in action witnessed in and through his life.

The words that we fill our minds and thoughts with will become part of us so that we also act and behave according to those words. The Bible speaks a lot about healing and so I want to uncover this message - to look at the healing ministry of the church and to seek out the healing miracles that can be released through biblical faith-centred thinking and speech.

There are many, many people who for one reason or another are seeking healing at this time. You may be one of those and it may be the reason that you are reading this book. I pray right now that God will open your heart so that as you search, seek and question how you can reach into God's healing love, your healing will be met. Jesus said:

Matthew 21:22

And whatever you ask in prayer, you will receive, if you have faith.

Do you believe that God will heal you?

I claim no special ability or power; I am simply seeking to tap in to the source of power that I know exists through God. I am acutely aware of the huge responsibility that this task entails. I am also very aware that the subject of healing has created on the one hand euphoria when healings taking place and on the other hand emotional pain when healing does not occur.

Before I go further, integrity is important. I am not going to try to hide or deny that there are many occasions when people have sought biblical (divine) healing. They have gone to healing church services or to people with healing ministries, but it simply has not worked. I have heard many church people and ministers trying to explain this, making excuses. These explanations often come from their own (genuine) attempts to find answers; sometimes they have misquoted or missed the point of scripture. I have also come across dear people who strongly defend their church and faith, stating simply that healings and miracles do take place whilst setting aside those many that have not. Others deny access to independent verification of healings. All of this has created confusion and judgment from the world looking in at a church that makes wild and unsubstantiated claims.

Dear friend, I am not trying to be critical or harsh. I am not trying to be disloyal to God or faithless. I am also not trying to criticise those in the healing ministry. I simply want to find out what affects or blocks healing from taking place and to investigate how the miracle power of biblical healing can be released as the natural process that the Bible indicates it should be. Unfortunately, instead of seeking out the 'why' we are all too often guilty of blaming God or making excuses such as "It was not God's will."

To illustrate what I mean, some thirty or so years ago I was invited to speak at a church. I chose to speak on the subject of healing. In those days this was quite new to the listeners of the congregation and it caused a few very uncomfortable reactions. One lady came to me after the service; she was really upset and told me in no uncertain terms that healing was not for everyone. I learned a very important lesson on that day. It does not matter how much faith I may have or what gifts God may give to me; without compassion I am nothing and, more importantly, without God I can do nothing. On that day my message was delivered out of good intent, but it lacked compassion and understanding of the hurts that people have encountered through poor teaching and insufficient love. I also realised that not having complete trust in God is one reason why we fail to see the power of God released. Sometimes this faith is released by the minister, sometimes by the receiver, and very often by both.

As mentioned earlier, the subject of divine healing has not only created much joy, happiness, belief and faith but also confusion, debate, hurt, disagreement and controversy. There will, of course, always be sceptics - people who will not accept anything to do with God or biblical faith even if they receive a miracle themselves. That is their personal choice and one that they are free and entitled to take, but what of those who through poor teaching and lack of understanding have been hurt?

Some years ago I had fringe experiences in the healing ministry of the church. It did not take me long to realise just how awesome the calling of the healing ministry is - not one to be taken lightly. Perhaps more than any other ministry of the church it leaves (or should leave) those engaged in it totally in the hands of God. The healing ministry is not supported or enhanced by an individual's natural gifts and abilities in terms of their intellect, oratory skills, personality or charisma. In ministering healing you are just a channel, but you have to be a channel of faith.

People came with needs about which I knew I could do nothing to help of my own ability even though my natural inclination was to see everyone healed. If I could have helped, I would have. I had, and still have, no such ability or power of myself, but I do know for a certainty that God has that powerful gift. I have seen this power in action, and I will share with you why I have this confidence through the example of George.

THE HEALING OF GEORGE

Before writing about this healing I carefully checked the details with George's wife. What I am about to write has been confirmed and is open to scrutiny.

George had suffered from a back problem which had been diagnosed as spondylosis of the lumbar region of his back - a degenerative condition causing severe pain and immobility. I asked George if he would like to receive healing to which he said 'yes'. I then asked God for George's healing. The pain stopped and George went back to his doctor for a scheduled appointment. The back was x-rayed and found to be clear. George went for many years with no problem in movement or pain. Working in the building trade George did cause a slight injury to his back a couple of years ago, but apart from a few twinges from this he remains fully recovered over thirty years later. God acted on George's faith and request for help in a small caravan whilst on holiday.

God's power is within all Christians, but the fact is, Christian or not, sickness knows no boundary, and there are even those who blame God for it. This blame culture is, as we will see, not new. In times of desperate need and in desperate situations it is not unreasonable to ask 'why'; it is not beyond the human psyche to seek a guilty cause or source. What we need to be sure of in dishing out a verdict and pointing a guilty finger is, have we got the right evidence and person?

Blaming God

The deception of blaming God or even going as far as to say that God has put an illness upon a person is one all too often used. The fickleness of our thinking is displayed when on the one hand we blame God for disasters and illnesses whilst on the other hand we do not credit God when miracles occur or healings take place. Instead we claim that they are natural phenomena - elements of nature or the result of our own positive thinking. In good times, some people will even declare that God does not exist.

It is a perfectly logical question to ask where sickness comes from; so let's take a while to investigate this. Pointing the finger at God concerning sickness is not new. The religious leaders at the time of Jesus, the Pharisees, attempted to say that Jesus himself was a cause. Jesus then answered this illogical and viciously conceived accusation. Let's examine the scenario and the response that was given.

Matthew 12:22-28

Then a blind and dumb demoniac was brought to him, and he healed him, so that the dumb man spoke and saw. And all the people were amazed, and said, 'Can this be the Son of David?' But when the Pharisees heard it they said, 'it is only by Beelzebul, the prince of demons, that this man casts out demons.' Knowing their thoughts, he said to them, 'Every kingdom divided against itself is laid to waste, and no city or house divided against itself will stand, and if Satan casts out Satan, he is divided against himself; how then will his kingdom stand? And if I cast out demons by Beelzebul, by whom do your sons cast them out? Therefore they shall be your judges. But if it is by the Spirit of God that I cast out demons, then the kingdom of God has come upon you.'

It was abundantly clear to all around that Jesus had not only healed a man but also cast out of him a demon that had possessed him. Satan was not casting himself out of the possessed man, and Jesus turned to address the Pharisees on this. They were unable to find an answer to the points that Jesus raised with them, and yet in their eyes he was still treated as guilty.

Nowhere can we find evidence in the Bible or historical documents to suggest that Jesus was anything other than a man who acted for the good of those around him. He healed many and provided for many. From the very beginning of the Bible and throughout we see that God's heart and purpose is for good:

Genesis 1:31

God saw everything that He had made, and behold, it was very good.

What ruined all of this was the deception of Satan described in Genesis 3:1-24. God never made us to be robots; we have free will, free thought and free actions. It was this free choice that led to a separation from God, for good and evil cannot reside together, but God has done everything possible to leave the door open for our return. This invitation is a matter for us, individually, to accept or reject.

In Acts we find revealed the source of sickness and much, much more:

Acts 10:38

God anointed Jesus of Nazareth with the Holy Spirit and with power;
how he went about doing good and healing all that were oppressed by the
devil, for God was with him.

Sickness is of the devil. When we realise what the source of sickness
is we know with confidence that we have a powerful remedy made
possible through the blood of Christ.

The challenge is for us to put away old prejudices, to question why
we believe what we believe and where these beliefs came from. Are the
beliefs that we hold ours or someone else's? How do these beliefs measure
up against what the Bible says?

We need to take responsibility for our own actions, our own
behaviour, and our own misuse of our bodies and the planet, rather than
to shift that blame so easily. Yes, there are natural occurrences of nature,
and we need to accept that they are natural occurrences - they are not of
God. The logic behind blaming God for bad and evil things that happen is
not compatible with His goodness, love and healing. John writes:

1 John 4:8

He who does not love does not know God; for God is love.

Followers of Christ are not only expected but also commanded to
love, just as God loves and just as Jesus demonstrated in his life. The very
example of love is before us. If we understand that God demands love
and acts in love then what is the logic in blaming God for being unloving?

The Source of Sickness

Until we fully grasp that sickness is not from God but rather from
Satan (a result of sin and oppression or evil spirit possession) we will never
fully break through into healing power. This statement - that Satan is the
author of sickness and disease - requires further explanation.

Where there is oppression, possession and domination, these are
sure signs that something is from Satan. I am not saying that a particular
person has necessarily been guilty of a particular sin and that this has

caused an illness. There are lots of good living people, Christian or otherwise, who suffer ill health. This is rather the result of sin in general, for we are all sinners and fall short of God's intention for us; it is one of the ways that Satan uses to oppress, dominate and deceive. Of course, some sickness can be caused directly by sins such as unforgiveness; these can upset the body systems, causing stress, anger and bitterness, raising blood pressure and disrupting the body's chemical processes etc.

Take a look at how many times the Bible points to the fact that there is a link between a sickness or illness and an evil spirit.

Mark 1:32-34

That evening, at sundown, they brought to him all who were sick or possessed with demons. And the whole city was gathered together about the door. And he healed many who were sick with various diseases, and cast out many demons.

In fact, Jesus was even more specific about the link between sickness and Satan when he was confronted about healing a woman on the Sabbath day. Let's take a closer look at this story in Luke 13:10-17. Here we read that Jesus was teaching and a woman who had been infirm for eighteen years was healed as Jesus spoke these words:

Luke 13:12

Woman, you are freed from your infirmity.

Unbelievable as it may sound and be, the ruler of the synagogue criticised Jesus for this act because it was on the Sabbath! Jesus responded by saying:

Luke 13:15,16

You hypocrites! Does not each of you on the Sabbath untie his ox or his ass from the manger, and lead it away to water it? And ought not this woman, a daughter of Abraham who Satan bound eighteen years ago, be loosed from this bond on the Sabbath day?

What do we learn from these verses?

- Jesus spoke and it was so (verse 12 – "You are freed from your infirmity").
- Jesus also laid his hands on the woman and she was immediately healed (verse 13).
- Satan had bound the woman in infirmity for eighteen years (verse 16 – "Satan bound for eighteen years").

Again we read Peter saying;

Acts 10:38

God anointed Jesus of Nazareth with the Holy Spirit and with power; how he went about doing good and healing all that were oppressed by the devil, for God was with him.

Jesus was anointed with the Holy Spirit and God's power to deal with Satan's oppression in sickness. How much more do *we* need to be anointed with the Holy Spirit and God's power?

James reminds us that evil is from Satan but goodness is from God.

James 1:13-17

Let no one say when he is tempted, 'I am tempted by God': for God cannot be tempted with evil and he himself tempts no one: but each person is tempted when he is lured and enticed by his own desire. Then desire when it has conceived gives birth to sin: and sin when it is full-grown brings forth death. Do not be deceived, my beloved brethren. Every good endowment and every perfect gift is from above, coming down from the Father of lights with whom there is no variation or shadow due to change.

God only gives what is good, and healing is an example of this good that we can tap into.

In the course of proclaiming the kingdom of heaven, Jesus also went about healing every kind of sickness and infirmity. Why? In the first letter of John we read:

1 John 3:8

The reason the Son of God appeared was to destroy the works of the devil.

Jesus came to destroy all that is of Satan. Separation from the kingdom of God is because of sin originating from Satan. Sickness and infirmity originate from Satan, and so Jesus has paved the way to destroy anything that is of Satan – that which blocks us from God's perfect will. In Exodus we read these words:

Exodus 15:26
I am the Lord, your healer.

So does this mean that healing is for everyone?

Is Healing For All?

This is a logical question to ask. In my view, it should also not be shirked; I am certainly not going to encourage positive thinking, speech, belief and faith in God based upon the avoidance of hard questions.

I would encourage you to carry out your own research, but I can find no reference in the Bible that says that healing is only for certain people or for certain illnesses. I can also find no reference to say that it is God's will that people should suffer illness. Of those that came to Jesus no one was turned away or not healed. For example we read:

Matthew 8:16
That evening they brought to him many who were possessed with demons; and he cast out the spirits with a word, and healed all who were sick.

Jesus healed *all* that were sick!

If we turn to Mark 9:21-24 we read the account of a demonic boy being healed. In verse 22 the boy's father says to Jesus, "If you can do anything, have pity upon us."

Obviously totally astounded by this statement we read in verse 23 Jesus saying, "*If* you can!" It is as if Jesus cannot believe what he had just heard. He goes on to say, "All things are possible to him who believes." All things are possible *to him who believes*. Who is this referring to? It is to anyone - available to everyone who believes. The belief that something will happen is open to every person, no matter who you are.

In faith we can come to Jesus, daring to believe that he will act on his promises. Healing is one of God's promises, activated through faith. Again in Luke 5:12 a man suffering from leprosy said to Jesus, "If you are willing, you can make me clean," and the response of Jesus was, "I am willing." There was no hesitation; Jesus wants the best for all of us. His will is that we are made whole.

In Mark 11 we read:

Mark 11:22

Have faith in God.

This is then followed by the following incredible words

Mark 11:23

Truly, I say to you, whoever says to this mountain, 'Be taken up and cast into the sea', and does not doubt in his heart, but believes that what he says will come to pass, it will be done for him.

Take a closer look again at this astounding statement which Jesus says is true. "Whoever says" - who is this 'whoever'? It is you and me! The statement is therefore aimed at everyone!

Dear friend, it is not a question of whether God is willing to heal. Nor does He offer healing to some but not others, as though He would have favourites. Healing is no more held back from anyone that seeks it than salvation is held back; they are both freely available to all. The question is, do you (do we, do I) really believe that God is true to His word? Do we truly and honestly trust God in everything?

To the question "Is healing for all?" the answer must be an emphatic "Yes!" If the question is changed slightly to "Are all healed?" the answer is clearly "No" in most of our church healing services and experiences today. Are there examples of people failing to be healed in the Bible? The answer is a qualified "No". In Matthew 17:14-20 we read of a boy suffering from epilepsy who was not healed by the disciples because of their lack of faith. The boy was, however, healed by Jesus.

We are undoubtedly confronted with a real issue.

Psalm 103:3

Who forgives all your iniquity, who heals all your diseases.

The death of Jesus was not just for salvation and forgiveness; it also opened the way to healing.

1 Peter 2:24

By His stripes you were healed.

To say that God's healing is not for all is like saying that God's forgiveness is not for all. In truth, just as forgiveness and salvation are for all, so healing is also for all. However, not all receive these because blockages exist. If I give someone who is special to me a gift that is operated by battery, it is given so that they can use it once the battery has been fitted. I do not give a gift that is broken and dysfunctional. In 1 Corinthians 12:1-11 we read that God has granted a variety of gifts, and in verse nine we discover that one of these gifts is the gift of healing. Now why would God provide a gift if it was of no use or dysfunctional? God provides the gift of healing so that it will be used. It is a gift that works as soon as we have connected the spiritual battery. I have to conclude therefore that healings are as relevant today as they were in the time of Christ. They should take place so what are the blockages?

The famous prayer 'The Lord's Prayer' found in Matthew 6:10-14 is recited so often by so many people, and yet the impact and the truths behind what we are actually saying are often missed. For example, let us look at it here in the context of healing. When we pray, "Your will be done on earth as it is in heaven," we are asking that God's will in heaven will also be available on earth. The will of God is for everyone and healing is a part of it. Not everyone, however, *wants* the will of God and that is a free and personal choice. "Is healing for all?" is not the correct question; rather, the question is "Are all for healing?"

Error in teaching blocks God's perfect plan, placing people in bondage to what they have come to believe. A related issue is that of attempting to compartmentalise God by placing Him into set boxes to fit our beliefs, traditions and actions. Just because we may have always done something in one particular way does not allow God to move as He wills.

Tradition can be a very limiting factor in our Christian living. Have you ever wondered why Jesus was not prescriptive in what he did? Why the healings that we read about are performed in so many different ways? Why we do not have set patterns and steps that show us how to get someone healed? Jesus made a very interesting point whilst speaking with his disciples, warning them against unbelief; he concluded by saying:

John 8:28, 29

When you have lifted up the Son of man, then you will know that I am he, and that I do nothing on my own authority but speak thus as the Father taught me. And he who sent me is with me; he has not left me alone, for I always do what is pleasing to him.

Jesus presumed nothing. He acted as he was led and did as he was given authority to do by God, keeping His commandments.

What I am trying to say here? Simply that it is important to check what the Bible has to say and to listen to God and obey His leading and His commandments. As well as the fact that Jesus did exactly this, the same message is encapsulated in the following words from John's first letter:

1 John 3:21-24

Beloved, if our hearts do not condemn us, we have confidence before God; and we receive from him whatever we ask, because we keep his commandments and do what pleases him. And this is his commandment, that we should believe in the name of his Son Jesus Christ and love one another, just as he has commanded us.

The early church demonstrated an unflinching commitment and belief in God, keeping His commandments and walking in holiness and the Holy Spirit.

Acts 5:12-16

Now many signs and wonders were done among the people by the hands of the apostles. And they were all together in Solomon's Portico. None of the rest dared join them, but the people held them in high honour. And more than ever believers were added to the Lord, multitudes both of men and women, so that they even carried out the sick into the streets, and laid them on beds and pallets, that as Peter came by at least his shadow might fall on some of them. The people also gathered from the towns around Jerusalem, bringing sick and those afflicted with unclean spirits, and they were all healed.

If we walk with God as the New Testament church did, these same signs and wonders will be evident today.

A TRIBUTE TO MARY (MAISIE) DOBNEY

It is important that in everything I am saying there is a balance, integrity and an understanding that God must be allowed to be God.

Mum Dobney, my wife's mother, had lived a life caring for others. She was a midwife and nursing sister specialising in difficult and premature births. At the age of 92 Mum Dobney collapsed and was taken into hospital. She had some twenty years beforehand suffered a massive heart attack but had recovered and lived a normal active life with the attitude of keeping fit and healthy and helping others until once again her heart began to falter.

Whilst in hospital she contracted *Clostridium difficile* and was extremely ill. Seeing the pain and discomfort that Mum Dobney was going through, my wife asked me to pray that God would allow her to die and end the misery. I began to seek God's will. I simply could not ask God to take this dear soul. I agreed with my wife that we would seek dignity and release from pain. The grace of God was such that Mum Dobney had relief from her pain. She was moved to the hospital in which she had ended her career - a place that she had so fondly talked about - and was placed in a private room with the same number as her small flat, as if she had come home. Mum Dobney died released from pain, in dignity and peacefully in her sleep.

By the grace of God our prayers, offered in faith, were answered.

Learning to Unlock Healing Miracles

Mark 11:22-25

Have faith in God. Truly I say to you, whoever says to this mountain, 'be taken up and cast into the sea', and does not doubt in his heart but believes that what he says will come to pass, it will be done for him. Therefore, I tell you, whatever you ask in prayer, believe that you have received it and it will be yours. And whenever you stand praying, forgive, if you have anything against any one, so that your Father also, whio is heaven, may forgive you your trespasses.

This text includes so many incredible statements, beginning with the invitation to have faith in God. (In Hebrews chapter 11 we learn why this is so important. We are told in verse six that it is impossible to please God without faith.) A truly powerful word is then spoken: it is a reliable, assured fact that whoever (that is you or me or anyone) does not doubt will certainly get what they ask for.

HEALING POWER OF FAITH

The first thing that we learn from this verse is where we should place our faith. The firm message here is that our faith should be placed in God, not in anyone or anything else. We then learn that faith will enable us to have the things we ask for, whilst doubt will be a hindrance. We also learn that everyone is included; there are no exceptions.

James tells us why doubt is so damaging:

James 1:6-8

But let him ask in faith without any doubting, for the one who doubts is like the surf of the sea driven and tossed by the wind. For let not that man expect that he will receive anything from the Lord, being a double-minded man, unstable in all his ways.

There are several example verses in the Bible that attribute healing directly to faith. Faith in God is required of whoever ministers divine healing, but it is not always a requirement of the person seeking healing.

HEALING POWER OF SPEECH

In our text from Mark 11 the importance of speaking is highlighted several times:

- "Whoever says" – 'Whoever' is an inclusive word; it leaves no one out.
- "Believes that what he says" – This is an encouragement to say what you believe and believe what you say.
- "Whatever you ask" – 'Whatever' is an inclusive word, and again the encouragement is to speak out.
- "Stand praying" – Prayer is again 'to speak'.

There are several references in the Bible that refer to the generic healing power of the words that we speak. In Proverbs we read:

Proverbs 12:18
The tongue of the wise brings healing.

Proverbs 15:4
A soothing tongue is a tree of life.

Proverbs 16:24
Pleasant words are a honeycomb, sweet to the soul and healing to the bones.

Great care should be taken over where our faith is rooted, what we believe, what we ask for and why we are asking. In James 3:1-18 the dangers of the tongue are outlined. Take a moment now to read this chapter.

Healings take place because...

- ...of God's love and compassion for mankind.
- ...of God's mercy toward mankind.
- ...Jesus paid the price for our healing on the cross.
- ...they are evidence of God's love and the price Jesus has already paid.
- ...they glorify God and bring people to faith in God.

HEALING POWER OF FORGIVENESS

Let's take a moment to understand why forgiveness is a key area in unlocking healing. When one is engaged in unforgiveness it creates in us a powerful emotional state which can affect our own health. Holding a grudge or resentment can lead to anger, stress, anxiety and depression. These prolonged states can in turn lead to headaches, high blood pressure, increased heart rate, stomach upsets and so on. These states can grow and create in us powerful destructive forces that can paralyse healing.

Illness is an imbalance or blockage of the natural energy flow of the body caused by disharmony in our thinking or external influences such as what enters our body. The body has a powerful defensive system, but this defence can be so unbalanced that it begins to work against itself; the cells and chemical balances of the body overproduce or destroy one another. Unforgiveness not only breaks a link with God but also with others and within our own selves. Unforgiveness is destructive, and that which is destructive will affect our health and healing.

Medical research is now finding a strong correlation between forgiveness and such things as lower blood pressure, lower pain and speed of recovery from injury or illness.

HEALING POWER OF PRAYER

James 5:14-15

Is any one of you sick? He should call the elders of the church to pray over him and anoint him with oil in the name of the Lord. And the prayer offered in faith will make the sick person well; the Lord will raise him up. If he has sinned, he will be forgiven.

This promise is also supported by the following fact:

Matthew 21: 22

Whatever you ask for in prayer believing, you will receive.

The problem that is often encountered is that prayers are not prayers of faith but of compromise. What I mean here is that instead of praying for specific healing believing that this will happen, the prayers move to words such as "give the person comfort", "remove their pain", "give their relatives strength", "help the doctors" and so on. These are the prayers that are prayed and believed; so this is exactly what is received in accordance with God's promise that "whatever you ask, believing, you will receive".

HEALING POWER OF CONFESSION

James 5:14-16
Confess your sins to each other and pray for each other so that you may be healed. The prayer of a righteous man is powerful and effective.

The thing to notice here is that it is the prayer of a righteous person that has power.

For many the meaning of the word 'confess' is 'to admit, to own up, to say sorry' but it can also mean 'to speak out and tell others about one's beliefs' or 'to tell others about a healing'. Jesus often combined teaching with healing. Those who were healed went and told others who flocked to Jesus. The greatest healing, of course, is that of a person's soul.

HEALING POWER OF ACTING IN GOD'S WILL

There were many times when I ministered healing that I found myself instinctively asking God for His permission. In those early days I did not really understand; I just asked.

Jesus makes a telling statement in John 5:

John 5:19
Truly, truly, I say to you, the Son can do nothing of his own accord, but only what he sees the Father doing; for whatever he does, that the Son does likewise.

Jesus did not presume anything. He even went as far as to say that he could do nothing of his own accord. What he did was what his father did. Jesus followed the lead of his father.

Any person or minister who engages in the healing ministry and does not realise that they have no gift or ability of their own (no open door or right of their own) deceives themselves and those around them.

It is for God to grant and for the person acting as God's channel to be exactly that - a channel acting in humility and obedience as God leads. There are times when we need to step back and remember that healing is not through our ability. It is not *our* ministry or *our* gift. If Jesus could do nothing of his own accord then we fool ourselves if we think we are different. We need to take time to ask God and then do what he says.

HEALING POWER OF PERSISTENCE

With God all things are possible; it is impossible for God to fail. All we need to do is believe. The signs and wonders that we see in the Bible and healings today exist so that we have evidence that God is who He says He is.

It is up to us to refuse anything other than God's promises, but sometimes receiving requires persistence. Take a look at Luke 11:5-13. In verse 9 we read:

Luke 11:9
Ask, and it shall be given to you, seek and you shall find; knock and, it shall be opened to you.

Healing Dilemma?

A little known and yet dynamic man of faith from Bradford, England called Smith Wigglesworth (1859 – 1947) once said:

I was very critical in my spirit and would judge people so harshly. I did not know why so many people who taught Divine Healing wore glasses. I questioned, "Why do you wear glasses if you believe in Divine Healing?" This stumbled me somewhat. Later I had to wear glasses to read my Bible, and I was often criticised for this.

Smith learned three things. Firstly that he had been critical; secondly that his critical nature had caused him to stumble; and thirdly that his critical thinking resulted in him wearing glasses. As I pondered this situation I became aware that what Smith had actually done, like so many of us, was to demonstrate pride that caused him to become critical. God hates pride. Was this as a salutary reminder to strengthen Smith?

I do not know why these people were not healed of their sight deficiencies. I also do not know why God does many things that He does. But I *do* know that He heals, that God must be trusted and that I must trust God to be God.

If we take a look at the Apostle Paul we learn in 2 Corinthians 12:7-10 that his affliction (we have no idea what this was) served to strengthen his service. This was explained to him as follows:

2 Corinthians 12:9

My grace is sufficient for you, for power is perfected through weakness.

I can understand that a person who is in service to God may need to be reminded of their place if, for example, they might become carried away with who they are. Here an affliction such as poor eyesight might serve as a reminder and perfecter of their faith. This is however a situation that rests between the individual and God, with the onus placed on the individual.

If I am to believe what God says about healing, I must conclude that if a healing does not take place then something is clearly wrong and that 'that something' is not resting at God's door. In other words, we need to look at ourselves. I am personally of the opinion that we should not accept ill health, sickness or disease. The Bible is clear that healing of the mind, spirit, disease, sickness, sight, lameness, epilepsy, leprosy and so on, did (and do) take place.

Stumbling

From my reading of the Bible and research of recorded healings I have, in all honesty, personally found no mention of amputees or those born with missing limbs being restored. I have read of some who say that Jesus healed those with leprosy and suggest that lepers will have had fingers, hands or feet that had fallen off restored. We must take care, dear friends; it is a man made myth that those suffering from leprosy lost fingers and limbs.

Healings of one form or another will take place but I cannot explain why some of these healings are internal and spiritual rather than also physical as in the case of amputees. Is this a good enough reason to stumble and to throw the 'baby out with the bath water'? Is it a good enough reason to say that healing is not God's will or not His will for all? Just because we can find no record to say that a person has 'grown' a new limb it does not mean that it has not happened or that it will never happen. Some people even say that if they see the miracle of a limb regrowing they will, and only then, believe in God. Yes, many certainly will believe at this sight, but there are still those who will not believe whatever they see before them.

These critics almost glibly pass on their doubts and excuses instead of taking personal responsibility. "I will not believe until I see," they say and then sit back and wait for others to act instead of trying for themselves. To see a miracle of such proportion as regrowth of a limb takes total and absolute faith. The disciples themselves were rebuked for failing to heal a boy with epilepsy. We have already discovered that doubt and fear block healings.

I for one confess my failings. Some years ago I was called to a hospital where a man had gone into a deep coma following a series of strokes. I went with a missionary who was home from Bolivia and who had visited many in hospital as part of his work in that country. He had seen many people healed in his hospital ministry.

We went to the bedside of this coma patient and we began to pray, seeking God for guidance and help. As we were praying, the man we were praying over suddenly sat bolt upright. I have never been so shocked and scared. I completely lost the plot at this stage, and the man gently lay back down. He died a few days later. My faith was tested that day and I did not, in all honesty, pass the test.

I have come across stories of those with healing ministries who have given up because a healing did not take place. I can understand the feelings and sentiment behind the anguish and pain these dear folk have been through. I do not know why this has happened; I cannot give an answer. But I do know that my faith in God is one of trust - that He knows better. I also know, as hard as this may sound, that it is not by my power or ability that a person is healed. My responsibility is to walk with God, to obey His commands, to listen and to act as God directs.

During the course of writing this book I have been searching God on these matters. During one such deliberation I became aware that I had been asking the wrong questions and approaching things from the wrong perspective.

CHANGING THE QUESTION

The question I should have been asking is "Why *does* God heal?" We turned our back on God and we fall short of any rights and priveleges. We have wanted free will to do as we please. We have destroyed parts of the earth and we cover our food in pesticides and so on. The little trick that we then play is to blame God. We are like naughty children who, when caught, deny involvement or push blame elsewhere and then, when given a sanction, say that our parents do not love us. When we are called to trust our parents we think that we know better and we do our own thing!

Healings are God's way of...

- ...reminding us that He is there.
- ...reminding us of His love.
- ...bringing people to the kingdom of heaven.
- ...allowing us room to trust Him.
- ...showing His mercy.

CHANGING THE PERSPECTIVE

Healing is not about my ability; it is about my faith and my trust in God. I do not own healing power. It is not mine to do with as I please. It is not mine to play with like a toy. Anyone involved in the healing ministry must understand that we deal with real people with real needs.

I would encourage you to take a look at the life of motivational speaker Nick Vujicic - a thirty year old man born with no legs or arms. Nick says:

Never give up. If you fail a hundred times, get up a hundred times. Having a disability does not mean that you cannot do something. What

stops many of us is our mind. We need to see what we do have and what
we can do.

Nick says of his physical disability that if God does not give you a miracle then you *are* a miracle if you trust Him. Nick has seen over 200,000 people become Christians through his ministry. He goes on to say:

Do not give up on God for God will not give up on you.

When we meet difficult situations and circumstances we have two choices. One is to give up and say that there is no point, to shift blame or even to go into denial. The second is to ask, "How can I overcome this problem? What are my responsibilities? And what can I do differently?"

Those that have learned how to live positive and successful lives know that there is no failure - there is only learning. The question should be "What can I learn and what can I do differently in this situation?" So let's take a hold of our responsibility and look at the question of healing from different viewpoints in order to see what we can learn and maybe do differently.

I want to make it clear again that I have no special abilities. I am an ordinary 'guy next door' type of person who, on top of that, is a habitual sinner - someone who has caused considerable hurt to others, not least of which his very own family. I have failed God many times through weakness and even sheer disobedience. I have sought different avenues in my life, but never have I found what my heart longs for deep down other than when I have come to God. Apart from the grace of God I am nothing, and I certainly deserve nothing of myself. Yet despite everything, God has never once given up on me.

Some years ago, during a difficult time of my life, I was walking around a swimming pool (between teaching swimming groups) to check the water and the area generally. I had walked one length and width of the pool talking to God using internal dialogue and had concluded that of course I did not deserve His help. As I turned to walk the second length, a voice, different from my own internal voice, said to me, "What makes you think that you are different from anyone else?" I stopped sharply, realising that God cared for me as much as He does anyone else. It was my choice to accept or reject God's grace and my choice to act or to carry on as I was - to trust or to disobey.

Blockages to Healing

I have struggled so many times to understand why it is that the Bible is so very clear about healing. Given what is said about healing throughout its pages, it just has to happen far more frequently and in a much more widespread way than is evident today.

My understanding regarding things that can block healing was sharpened when my wife was diagnosed with a Spigelian hernia, requiring keyhole surgery. I sought God for this healing, and my wife reported back to me that as I had prayed she had felt tremendous heat coming from me and that the pain and uncomfortableness of the hernia had subsided.

I have to tell you that my wife still required that surgery. You may ask why; I certainly did. But as I sought answers I realised that it was due to several shortcomings in me.

LACK OF FAITH

The revelation that I lacked faith came as a surprise to me at first, but I began to read through Mark's Gospel. The first few chapters are covered with accounts of healings. I then came to chapter four, and in verse forty a telling comment was made by Jesus to his disciples.

The disciples were out at sea whilst Jesus lay sleeping, and we are told that a fierce gale arose. Remember that many of the disciples were fishermen so from their reactions the storm must have been bad.

Now, we know from the opening chapters that these men had seen Jesus perform some amazing healings. They were firsthand witnesses, there in person seeing what Jesus could do, and yet fear and doubt overtook their faith to the point where Jesus was obviously very surprised and said:

Mark 4:40

Why are you so timid [afraid]? How is it that you have no faith?

We read again in Matthew 14:22-33 how doubt blocked faith in the story of Peter walking on water toward Jesus. He was okay until he took his eyes off Jesus and looked at what the wind was doing. His faith was overcome and he was thwarted by doubt.

Yet again we read in Matthew 13:58 that Jesus did not do many works in Nazareth because of the lack of belief of the people.

I realised, being honest with myself, that doubts had begun to creep into my thinking regarding my wife's healing. I had moved from faith to hope tinged with a few moments of doubt.

Fear and doubt are major blockages in our thinking, and this in turn impinges on what we dare to do or to believe. They shift our trust and weaken our resolve, stopping us from doing and achieving. If we do not trust that something will work then we usually do not do it – a natural, protective reaction. Clearly my faith and trust when tested so simply (unlike the disciples) was left wanting.

The signs of healing were there for my wife, but through my lack of faith the healing flow was blocked and halted.

DOUBT

Doubt is when one is uncertain and unbelieving, leaving a person lacking confidence. This was exactly where I was, deep down. Instead of belief in my heart, there was doubt.

The opposite to doubt is certainty and belief - states that leave people in confidence. I did not have that inner conviction and confidence. As we have already discovered, lack of faith is also tied closely to doubt and lack of belief. Take a look at these statements:

Mark 9:23

All things are possible to him who believes.

Matthew 21:21

I tell you the truth, if you have faith and do not doubt.

Mark 11:24

Therefore I tell you, whatever you ask for in prayer, believe that you have received it, and it will be yours.

James 1:6,7

But let him ask in faith with out any doubting, for the one who doubts is like the surf of the sea driven and tossed by the wind. For let not that man expect that he will receive anything from the Lord.

It is clear to see the damaging effects of doubt in the context of healing.

UNFORGIVENESS

We have already investigated the importance of forgiveness. There are several reminders in the Bible about both forgiving others and also asking for forgiveness.

James 5:16

Therefore confess your sins to each other and pray for each other so that you may be healed. The prayer of a righteous man is powerful and effective.

Here we learn that the prayers of a righteous person are not only powerful but also effective. I was praying as an unrighteous man, having launched straight into praying for healing without first dealing with my own sinfulness and need for forgiveness. There was no power or effectiveness behind my prayer because I was not able to tap the source. My relationship had been affected much like the child who disobeys a parent leaving temporary disharmony and denial of privileges.

ARROGANCE AND FAMILIARITY

I am ashamed before God to admit a certain level of arrogance. In the spirit in which I have written this book (that is, one of self-learning and openness) I am sharing this so that others do not fall into the same trap as I.

There are times when we either blindly or with the best will in the world launch out into praying for the sick yet forget to come to God first or act from a weak prayer life and walk with God. This is how I occasionally acted. Dear friends, I am not trying to point a finger, but if

184

this is the way in which we are acting then it is time to take stock and remember who we are and who we are hurting in the process.

Another problem is that many churches simply treat healing a bit like a conveyor belt of prayer requests - going through the actions and ticking the boxes of things to do or, perhaps worse still, ignoring healing needs completely. We can find ourselves becoming 'familiar' with God. Now of course, familiarity in our walk with God can be a good thing in the sense that we grow closer to Him. However, if we develop familiarity and disregard of God's authority ('breeding contempt' as the saying goes) these can end up blocking the opportunity for God to work; His authority has been watered down. Take a moment to consider what had happened to Jesus in his home town of Nazareth:

Mark 6:4-6

'A prophet is not without honour, except in his own country, and among his own kin, and in his own house.' And he could do no mighty work there, except that he laid hands upon a few sick people and healed them. And he marveled because of their unbelief.

The question to ask ourselves - if we are honest, brave and bold enough - is what position does God have in our lives? Have service, good works, tradition or anything else taken over from God?

Healing Ministry

At the beginning of this chapter I invited you to investigate how Jesus went about healing the sick. I can think of no better way to look at the healing ministry than through the example that Jesus set.

In this short section I will speak of the healing ministry and those who operate in this ministry. Let us not be deceived. Just because a person claims a healing ministry and some people are healed it does not mean that this is truly blessed and anointed by God.

The healing ministry is not a game; it is not a spectacle or a road show. To treat it this way or, worse still, to expect or make money from this precious ministry is ungodly. It is not about an individual bringing adoration to themselves but rather about walking in the Spirit with love, humility and faith. This attitude of mind is no better illustrated than in Acts where we come across Peter and John going to the temple and on their way healing a lame man:

Acts 3:11-16

While he clung to Peter and John, all the people ran together to them in the potico called Solomon's, astounded. And when Peter saw it he addressed the people, 'Men of Israel, why do you wonder at this, or why do you stare at us, as though by our own power or piety we had made him walk? The God of Abraham and of Isaac and of Jacob, the God of our fathers, glorified his servant Jesus, whom you delivered up and denied in the presence of Pilate, when he had decided to release him. But you denied the Holy and Righteous One, and asked for a murderer to be granted to you, and killed the Author of life, whom God raised from the dead. To this we are witnesses. And his name, by faith in his name, has made this man strong whom you see and know; and the faith which is through Jesus has given the man this perfect health in the presence of you all.'

When the healing ministry of William Branham was brought to an abrupt end after he was tragically killed in a car accident by the reckless driving of a drunk, some people believed that he would rise from the dead - such was the power of his ministry. I am not attempting to belittle this - he was indeed a mighty man of God whom God blessed and greatly gifted. But it was not Branham who had the power in himself; it was from God. Branham would have said quite clearly and emphatically that he had no ability of his own; it was totally God-given. He was simply a willing and open channel.

Healing is about glorifying God. It is about bringing the evidence of God's love, His very heart and being to people so that they may see the kingdom of heaven. It is about His love for people to bring them to salvation. It is not about any one person, whoever they are. I know from my own experience of the healing ministry that it does not take long to realise just how helpless and vulnerable one feels. There are people with incredible needs, but I have no ability of myself to help them, much as my heart cries for them. The only thing I can do is whatever God says in the way in which He leads. Those engaged in the healing ministry should never be content with their own health and healing but rather have a heart that is stirred to see health and healing in everyone. The church, by the same token, must never be content with its own health and healing; it should be taking this gift to everyone, expecting it to be released to everyone.

Those with a healing ministry are inspired by God and manifest the Holy Spirit for the good of everyone.

1 Corinthians 12:6-9

There are varieties of working, but it is the same God who inspires them all in every one. To each is given the manifestation of the Spirit for the common good. To one is given, through the Spirit the utterance of wisdom, and to another the utterance of knowledge according to the same Spirit, to another faith through the same Spirit, to another gifts of healing by the one Spirit.

The mark of a ministry in healing is someone who is walking with God, in prayer and in the Holy Spirit, anointed by God. The same evidence that was seen through Jesus will manifest itself. Let's take a look at some of these signs:

- Matthew 4:23,24 – Every kind of disease and sickness will be healed, alongside teaching and proclamation of the gospel. The news will travel.
- Matthew 8:3 – Healing will take place by a simple touch.
- Matthew 8:8 – Healing will take place even if the person is not present and through the faith of another.
- Matthew 9:20,14:6 – Healing will takes place even through touching the healing minister's clothing.
- Matthew 11:5 – The dead will be raised.
- Matthew 15:28, John 5:8 – Healing will take place through speaking.
- Acts 5:15,16 – The shadow of a minister will be enough to heal the sick.

Unless God says otherwise, there is no hype, no 'show', no heavy laying on of hands, shouting and pushing. A simple touch is enough, though even this should be done under the guidance of the Holy Spirit and not in haste (1 Timothy 5:22). Great damage and injustice can be caused unless the Holy Spirit works through those walking in the Spirit. There is no need to get 'worked up'. The evidence of a healing ministry is that verifiable healings will take place - not as isolated incidents but as a natural part of the ministry. The simple fact of faith is that people will be healed.

Without love, compassion and a vulnerability that rests totally on faith in God, great damage can be caused by those who claim a healing ministry that is not anointed by God. No man has the right to claim his own ability to heal the sick. There are many false ministries and teachings, and Matthew tells us what to look out for:

Matthew 7:16
You will know them by their fruits.

Deception

The Bible frequently uses the picture of the sheep and the wolf, warning that we must be careful of the wolf (the evil one) who seeks to devour, to deceive and to prevent us from attaining the good things that are available to us.

The best deceptions are those that are very close to the truth - almost undetectable but sufficient to steer us off course.

Paul warned the Corinthian church about deceit and those who even disguise themselves as having a 'Christian' ministry:

1 Corinthians 11:14,15
Even Satan disguises himself as an angel of light. So it is not strange if his servants also disguise themselves as servants of righteousness. Their end will correspond to their deeds.

Some years ago I gave a series of talks about the healing ministry as part of an adult course open to anyone. The audience ranged from people interested in healing from a general perspective to some church people (including a few Roman Catholic nuns) and even a couple of 'faith healers'. One of the questions that a 'faith healer' asked me was how much I charged for each healing session.

Let's deal with these points so that no confusion can remain. Please understand that 'faith or spiritualist healing' is packaged to look and sound like the healing ministry of God. It feeds on the vulnerability of people who are desperate. Do faith healers see healings? Yes - to a point. Is it of God? No, most certainly not. It is a deception of Satan, offering and enticing people with healing but stealing from them eternal life.

The genuine healing ministry will be characterised as follows:

- The person ministering healing has, and claims, no healing power of their own.
- Jesus Christ is central to all that is said and done.
- The love and compassion of Jesus Christ is evident.
- No money is asked for, expected or taken.
- The Holy Spirit is central to the healing process. (Beware of meetings that simply stir up emotions.)

The logical question to ask is "How can we know that we are following the truth and not being deceived?" In the introduction to this book I began by saying that there can be no substitute for the Bible and I quoted the words of Smith Wigglesworth. In Acts 17 we learn that the Apostle Paul, along with Silas, went to a place called Beroea, an ancient city not too far from Thessalonica (now a town called Veria) to preach the gospel.

Acts 17:11

Now these Jews were more noble than those in Thessalonica, for they received the word with eagerness, examining the scriptures daily to see if these things were so.

What a wonderful example for us to follow. These people were eager to hear about God and Jesus, but they not only heard from Paul, they checked what the scriptures were saying. A salutary warning is given to us in the first letter to Timothy:

1 Timothy 4:1,2

Now the Spirit expressly says that in later times some will depart from the faith by giving heed to deceitful spirits and doctrines of demons, through the pretensions of liars whose consciences are seared.

The message is clear: accept the taught word of God but check the teaching against what the Bible actually says.

There are many distractions and 'good ideas' that can pull us away from the simple truth that faith in God unlocks healing; it is a faith and belief that comes from our heart - a total assurance and trust. Unbelief, even of the smallest amount, hinders healing; failing to seek forgiveness and God's guidance before praying for healing is a recipe for untold hurt.

In closing this chapter a thought crossed my mind. "How far have we diverged from the compass direction leading to our God-destination? Are we walking true north toward God?"

Epilogue

Many people think that God is in charge and controls the world. This, dear friend, is one of many deceptions - a mistaken and costly view. Jesus did not deny Satan's reign over the world when Satan tempted him.

Matthew 4:8,9

Again, the devil took him to a very high mountain, and showed him all the kingdoms of the world and the glory of them, and he said to him, 'All these I will give to you, if you will fall down and worship me.'

Yes, the death of Jesus has destroyed the power of Satan but Satan can still go where he wills to tempt, deceive and bring disease on those whom he chooses. Those who fail to come under the blood of Christ will be taken in by these things. If we think otherwise, it can stop us from seeing the glory of God, His power and promises flowing because we get into the mode of thinking that we can sit back. We think that God has it in control instead of actively inviting God to act and mobilising every part of our being to ensure that God is given a free reign. Yes, I am saying that we need to humble ourselves and give God total control - to offer ourselves that God may do with us as He wills for His glory. How often have we spoken the words of the Lord's Prayer but not fully grasped what it means? We have here an invitation for God's will to be done on earth as it is in heaven. These words need to take on a new and purposeful meaning.

God is not in control of the world. Man made a decision that he did not want God; he wanted to exercise his free will and separate from God. That was the point of the Adam and Eve story. As Christians, we can either live in the flesh, defeated, or in the Spirit, triumphant.

We have to mentally, physically and spiritually invite God into our lives. We have to invite Him to take us, mould us and use us. We have to invite Him to work His works. Faith is about allowing God to be free to act. Prayer is about a relationship and inviting God to work in our lives and in the world. Love is about having such a trust in God that we can relax, safe in His hands and care. Healing is about ridding Satan from our bodies and allowing God, through His Holy Spirit, to fill every part, every crevasse. And holiness is about renewing our minds, letting go and walking daily with God so that God's name, God Himself, is glorified.

There is a need for us individually to let go of ourselves, let go of our old thoughts and old beliefs and to say to God, "I am yours. Do with me as you will." This is not something that can be done lightly; it is not something that can be done half-heartedly. It is a conscious, wilful act on our part - letting go of our free will to act according to God's will. To live any other way is to dishonour God, the cross and that which Jesus sacrificed for us.

This act will invoke an answer. Many years ago I said to God, "I will do whatever you want and go wherever you wish." Within an hour my telephone rang, and a friend said to me that they knew a missionary in Botswana who was looking for people to go and help with their work. I was totally stunned but invited the missionary to come and talk with me. For various reasons it was clear that I was not called to actually go to Botswana. I was, however, tested by God on that day. Would I actually do as He said and wanted?

The invitation that we give to God must be serious, but without it we will never know His precious promises and live in His fulness.

God calls...

Isaiah 6:8
Then I heard the voice of the Lord saying, 'Whom shall I send? And who will go for us?'

What is your response? Isaiah was clear about where he stood on this question.

And I said, 'Here am I. Send me!'

Pursuing and Attaining Holiness

It is as if Peter would have himself written a concluding section to this book for me when we read:

1 Peter 1:13-16

Therefore, prepare your minds for action; be self-controlled; set your hope fully on the grace to be given you when Jesus Christ is revealed. As obedient children, do not conform to the evil desires you had when you lived in ignorance. But just as he who called you is holy, so be holy in all you do; for it is written: 'Be holy, because I am holy.'

Have you ever said to yourself something along the lines of "I would like to be like that person but I do not have their gift or talent"? Many Christian people have limited themselves by looking at others and how wonderful they are. When we do this it is easy to then say to ourselves, "I cannot attain that." It is so easy to look at the Wigglesworths, Branhams and Mullers and feel that they are untouchable. You and I are not these people; we are not supposed to judge ourselves or convict ourselves by their standards. Please do not misunderstand me; I am not saying that we cannot and should not want to be men and women of love, faith and prayer. But we do need to be who we are and to grow from where we are, with Christ as our role model, the Bible as our guide and the Holy Spirit as our comforter.

Many have fallen into the trap of comparing themselves with great people of God and concluding that they cannot attain holiness. Please, stop! This is not what the Bible says. Thinking this way is a deception, aimed at knocking us off balance and causing us to walk several steps behind God rather than with Him. I would urge you to allow this to sink into your spirit. Holiness is not something that is unattainable. If it were, the Bible would not so frequently call us to be holy.

1 Peter 1:16

As he who called you is holy, be holy yourselves in all your conduct; since it is written, you shall be Holy, for I am Holy.

For many people, holiness simply requires a fresh look at old habits and old ways of thinking. If you are not convicted in your life, if you are not convicted in your church, then dear friend, start asking God why. For many of us, our current living, church life and worship have something missing. It may be a lost direction, teaching that is not Spirit-inspired, habits and traditions, or even what I call a 'road show' church mentality - a lot of hype but little hard evidence.

Please understand me; I am not trying to criticise anyone or any form of worship. I am only interested in what God's word has to say and to walk in those ways. This may require us to turn away from the old habits that limit us and to long to be in the presence and arms of God, to be holy. In Mark 7:5-13 we read that Jesus makes a very powerful statement about traditions. The Pharisees are caught up in traditions and Jesus calls them hypocrites (verse 6). Jesus then goes on to say in verse 13 that tradition makes the word of God ineffectual! Take a closer look at that passage of scripture and check it out with the Holy Spirit. Being caught up in tradition takes the power behind the Word of God away! If you are wondering where the power has gone, take a look at how traditions have taken centre stage.

Conclusion

Holiness is about being set apart - separated so that God can use us in and for whatever purpose He wants. In 1 Thessalonians 3:13 we are called to establish ourselves in holiness. In other words, we are called to step up to God's level.

Hebrews 12:14

Pursue peace with all men, and holiness, without which no one will see the Lord.

Our call is to pursue and establish ourselves in holiness.

The title of this book is 'The Language of Love, Forgiveness, Faith, Prayer and Healing'. The message behind each life experience that we have looked at is about what we allow to enter our minds, what we think about, how this shapes our beliefs and faith and how what we think is demonstrated through our actions. In short, we are what we think. What are your thoughts at this moment in time?

Holiness is about us setting ourselves apart from traditions, setting ourselves apart from those, or that, which are not of God. It is an attitude of mind. It is about renewing what we think about so that it is in line with God's will and subsequently doing His will as we walk in the Spirit.

I cannot end this book more appropriately than to refer to the words opening Romans 12:

Romans 12:1,2

I beseech you therefore, brethren, by the mercies of God, that you present your bodies a living sacrifice, holy, acceptable to God, which is your reasonable service. And do not be conformed to this world, but be transformed by the renewing of your mind, that you may prove what is that good and acceptable and perfect will of God.

The vision of Chasing Your Dreams and Renewed Life Healing Ministries is to open a dedicated international centre where the work of God through health, fitness, healing and holiness will flourish as well as ministering to the community.

Contact us now with your request or questions:
Email: info@chasingyourdreams.co.uk
Visit our web site at www.chasingyourdreams.co.uk

Conclusion

From the Publisher

Titles in the **Timeless Teaching** series:

1.	What do These Stones Mean?	*Joyce Sibthorpe*
2.	Motherhood	*Diana Jeffery*
3.	A Walk with Wisdom	*Luke Jeffery*
4.	Four Mountains to Climb Before you Die	*Mark Jeffery*
5.	Can You Hear God?	*Joyce Sibthorpe*
6.	The Christian Guide to Jobs and Careers	*Charles Humphreys*
7.	Alive for a Purpose	*Kofi Owusu*
8.	Equipped to Heal	*Dr. Ian Andrews*
9.	Diagnosing Ills and Ailments of Relationships	*Adedeji Majekodunmi*
10.	Pursuing Holiness	*Sam Masamba*
11.	Single without Sinking	*Shade Vaughan*
12.	Redeeming a Nation	*Philip Quenby*
13.	Calling Things that Are Not as though They Were	*Barb Witt*
14.	Feasting on the Father	*Bill Smith*
15.	The Langue of Love, Forgiveness, Faith, Prayer and Healing	*Leon Gosiewski*

Books available from the publisher:
www.onwardsandupwards.org